EASTERN LITURGIES

IS VOLUME

112

OF THE

Twentieth Century Encyclopedia of Catholicism

UNDER SECTION

X

THE WORSHIP OF THE CHURCH

IT IS ALSO THE

42ND

VOLUME IN ORDER OF PUBLICATION

Edited by HENRI DANIEL-ROPS of the Académie Française

EASTERN LITURGIES

By IRENÉE-HENRI DALMAIS, O.P.

Translated from the French by DONALD ATTWATER

HAWTHORN BOOKS · PUBLISHERS · *New York*

First Edition, May, 1960

CONTENTS

INTRODUCTION

The bringing together of East and West is one of the most urgent tasks of the time in which we live. And an element of the very first importance in this task is a meeting and reconciliation between the great Christian traditions which, through the process of history, have for so long lived in ignorance and misunderstanding of one another.

It is in the Church's liturgy of worship, the official expression of her public prayer, that there may best be found the wealth of her tradition, stamped with the particular spirit of this or that civilization and history.

For some time now migration has brought about the establishment of communities of Christians of Eastern rites in Western Europe and the Americas. Religious services of these rites are more and more frequently celebrated in Roman-rite churches; radio, television, the gramophone enable more and more people to learn something about this unknown religious treasure. In many parts of North America, Eastern Christians, whether Orthodox or others or Catholics, are a familiar phenomenon, though still a little understood one. In Great Britain there are old-established and more recent communities of Orthodox and Armenians; and since 1945 there are several permanent churches of Slav-Byzantine Catholics.

The aim of this book is to be a first introduction to this little-known world, and it endeavours to give its right place to each of the liturgical traditions of the Christian East. It is true that the Byzantine rite is exceptionally important from every point of view. It is the expression of a Church whose mission it has been to safeguard and stand up for orthodoxy of faith in the great mysteries of the Trinity and the Incarnation and its liturgy sets forth that faith with an incomparable precision and depth which justly merit for it the name of the Orthodox Liturgy. For centuries Constantinople was the heart of an empire which claimed the title of ecumenical, universal; and this historic destiny made the Byzantine rite heir to the liturgical traditions of the older Churches of Jerusalem and of Antioch, of Asia Minor and of Greece, while missionaries handed it on, translated into their languages, to most of the Slav peoples, to the Rumanians and to the uttermost parts of Russian Asia.

But this glory must not lead us to neglect the other liturgies: the Syrian rites, expressions of a tradition which has continued to be more immediately nourished from Semitic roots, which, too, has planted vigorous shoots in India; and the Coptic rite, full of the spiritual experience of Egypt's monks and, through Ethiopia, deeply rooted in the land of Africa.

As full translations of the original texts are not always easy to come by, it has been thought desirable to quote, so far as limited space allows, the most important formulas of each liturgy. It is hoped that the reader will thus be enabled more fruitfully to take part in the pertinent celebrations when opportunity offers: for only such participation can lead to a real understanding of an action in which the Church 'lives out' her own mystery—a human community of which the living and effective Word of God, expressing itself in sacramental rites, makes the mystical Body of Christ.

TABLE OF EASTERN LITURGIES TODAY

ANTIOCHENE

The primitive Greek liturgy of Antioch later adopted certain usages proper to Jerusalem. From it derive in part the present:

(i) *(West) Syrian rite*. This is used in Syriac and some Arabic by the Jacobites and (West) Syrian Catholics of Syria, Lebanon and Iraq; in Malayalam by the Jacobites and Malankarese Catholics in India.

(ii) *Maronite rite*. A variant of the above, very "latinized" in some respects; used only by the Maronite Catholics of Lebanon and Syria, in Syriac with some Arabic.

BYZANTINE

The liturgy of Constantinople (Byzantium) is the result of many influences, notably those of Antioch and Jerusalem. The *Byzantine rite* is now used by all the Orthodox Churches and by the Catholic Melkites, Ruthenians (Ukrainians, etc.), Rumanians and others. Principal languages: Greek, Slavonic, Rumanian, Arabic.

ARMENIAN

The special liturgy of the Church of Armenia arose from a combination of Syrian and Cappadocian elements, within a framework taken from Jerusalem. In course of time it was modified by Byzantine and Latin influences. The *Armenian rite* of today is used both by the dissident Church and the Catholic minority, in the classical form of the Armenian language.

EAST SYRIAN

The people of Mesopotamia were evangelized mainly from Antioch, and their liturgy, still very archaic, seems to have taken shape at Edessa. It is now represented by:

    (i) the *Chaldean* or *East Syrian rite*. This is used, in Syriac, by the Nestorians in Iraq, Persia and Syria and by the Chaldean Catholics, mostly in Iraq.

    (ii) the *Malabar rite*. This form of the above is in some ways extremely "latinized". It is used only by the Syro-Malabarese Catholics of India, in Syriac.

ALEXANDRIAN

The original Greek liturgy of Alexandria, translated into Coptic (Egyptian), underwent strong monastic and Syrian influences, and subsequently was further revised and reformed. It is now known as:

    (i) the *Coptic rite*. This is the liturgy of the indigenous Christians of Egypt and their small Catholic minority. Coptic is its normal language, but a good deal of Arabic has been introduced.

    (ii) *Ethiopic rite*. The liturgy of the national Church of Ethiopia and of a small body of Catholics is a close relative of the above. It is celebrated in Ge'ez, now a dead language.

CHAPTER I

THE EASTERN CHURCHES: WHERE, WHEN

Christians of the West are sometimes surprised to learn that there is not one single Eastern Church but a number of Eastern Churches, each with a liturgy and other characteristics of its own, and that two or more of these Churches often overlap one another in the same territory: there are, for instance, three Catholic patriarchs with the title of Antioch (Melkite, Syrian, Maronite) and two dissident ones (Orthodox, Syrian Jacobite), not to speak of a Latin-rite titular prelate with the same title. In such cities of the Near East as Cairo and Aleppo there may be half a dozen bishops of different rites and obediences, though Christians form only a minority of the population.

So before approaching the Eastern liturgies it is necessary to make a brief historical survey, in order to understand the origins of these Churches and the far-reaching causes of their present situation.

During the first three centuries of our era the Christian communities formed a constellation within which a preponderating importance was recognized in the great apostolic sees of Rome, Antioch and, very soon, Alexandria; these were, moreover, the chief cities of the Roman empire and the centres of large administrative areas. This twofold aspect, religious and civil, was to have serious consequences in the course of time. While Roman tradition recognized primacies only in

Churches of apostolic foundation, the East attached much weight to the political status of cities; and councils at which Eastern representatives were in a majority gave the highest place after Rome to the later see of Constantinople, the New Rome (canon 28 of the Council of Chalcedon in 451, a canon which Pope Leo I refused to ratify). The see of Jerusalem, which was ranked among these patriarchates from the Chalcedon council onwards, never had the importance of the others from a hierarchical point of view; on the other hand, the spiritual prestige of the Holy City as a great centre of pilgrimage and monastic life carried its liturgical influence far and wide.

Beyond the frontiers of the Roman empire, the bishop of Seleucia-Ctesiphon, Papa bar Aggai, at the beginning of the fourth century sought to bring together the Churches of Mesopotamia under his own authority; they were reorganized within the Sassanian Persian empire at the Council of Seleucia in 410, after the violent persecutions under King Shapur II. Fourteen years later these Churches proclaimed themselves independent of the patriarch of Antioch and the ecclesiastical authorities of the Roman world; but at the same time they affirmed their fidelity to the faith of Nicaea. This secession was at first purely administrative; but little by little it developed into a state of schism which cut off the catholicate[1] of Seleucia-Ctesiphon from the rest of Christendom (Council of Beth Lapat, 484). The same thing happened in Armenia. Evangelized by missionaries who came, some from Eastern lands of Syriac speech, others, with St Gregory the Enlightener, from hellenized Asia Minor, this country was partitioned between the empires of Rome and Persia, and developed an acute consciousness of its lost unity and individuality. In 390 the catholicos Isaac the Great, son of the catholicos Narses I, broke the last links of Armenian dependence on the mother Church of Caesarea in Cappadocia. He entrusted the transla-

---

[1] The title of *catholicos*, in use in several churches, became equivalent to "patriarch". [*Trans.*]

tion into Armenian of the Bible and the great patristic writings
to a group which was led by the monk Mesrob, the inventor
of the Armenian alphabet. Sent to collect Syriac texts, two
members of this group, Joseph and Eznik, became acquainted,
probably at Edessa, with the liturgical usages of Jerusalem,
and these furnished the framework for the Armenian rite.
The neighbouring country of Georgia (Iberia), on the other
hand, after a period of fluctuation, came definitely into the
orbit of Constantinople.

The first evangelizers of the Ethiopians in the kingdom of
Axum also seem to have come from Syria, but Roman Syria;
however, they set themselves from the beginning to put their
converts under the metropolitan authority of Alexandria, and
this ecclesiastical bond conditioned the development of the
Ethiopian liturgy.

Thus in the middle of the fifth century, despite the disturb-
ances and sometimes schisms provoked by disputes about the
doctrine of the Holy Trinity (Councils of Nicaea, 325, and
Constantinople, 381) and about Christology (Council of Ephesus, 431), the Church appeared to be solidly and harmoniously
organized. Within the Roman empire there were five patriarchates: of these, Rome, Alexandria, Antioch and Jerusalem
were of apostolic origin, and were currently likened to the
four rivers of Paradise that refreshed and fertilized the earth
(Genesis 2. 10). The fifth see, at the imperial capital, Constantinople, put in a claim for foundation by the apostle St
Andrew who, says St John in his Gospel (12. 22), brought
some Greeks to Jesus. However disputable this claim may
be, the political importance of the city was worth a special
place for it in the ecclesiastical organization. Outside the
imperial borders, the catholicates of Persia and Armenia
had declared themselves independent (autocephalous), but
they had remained within the communion of the Catholic
faith.

Nevertheless, the balance was uneasy and already
threatened by cracks in the structure: these were continually

being widened by national aspirations, which the rather ineffective imperial administration found it more and more difficult to deal with, and by doctrinal divergences that emerged from the differences of mentality and culture that were still real and alive beneath a Greco-Latin veneer. Personal and institutional rivalries between the chief hierarchs and their sees, even when they were otherwise holy men, eventually led to irreparable breaches. To get a just idea of the sad period from the Council of Chalcedon in 451 to the Moslem expansion in the seventh century, for which that period had unconsciously prepared, it is important to have an inclusive mental picture of the factors involved, which were very various in kind and weight.

The condemnation of Nestorius by the Council of Ephesus led to tension, which was, however, soon relaxed by the wisdom of St Cyril of Alexandria († 444). But the condemnation of Eutyches at Chalcedon (and he was a man of much less weight than Nestorius) made the Chalcedonian doctrine a matter of terrible discord.

DIVISIONS AMONG THE EASTERN CHURCHES

The Nestorian Church

Whilst an excessively literal following of St Cyril's theological teaching was leading towards the monophysite schisms within the Roman empire, the Church of Persia, too exclusively attached to Antiochene theology and anxious to keep the Churches of the Roman world at their distance, defined its faith at the Council of Beth Lapat in 484. The formulas adopted were not incompatible with the Catholic faith; but they were rejected by the bishops in the Roman world, who alleged their too great dependence on the Antiochene teachers Diodore of Tarsus and Theodore of Mopsuestia. Now in Persia Theodore was regarded as the biblical interpreter *par excellence*, and Nestorius had been a disciple of his. Thus the

Persian Church became finally isolated in schism, and was henceforth known as Nestorian.[2]

The Monophysite Churches

At this time Roman imperial policy, caught between the divergent theological currents of Alexandria and Antioch, aimed above all at ensuring religious unity for the sake of maintaining the fragile cohesion of the empire. But its clumsy methods only made disagreement worse, especially when the emperor–theologian Justinian I († 565) found his ecclesiastical policy opposed by the empress Theodora, who supported the anti-Chalcedonians. The personality of the patriarch of Antioch Severus († 538) and the organizing ability of Jacob Baradai, whom Theodora had sent secretly into Syria in 543, brought about the formation of a Church at Antioch which rejected communion with those bishops who supported the orthodox faith of Chalcedon: this new body adopted the ambiguous formula "There is only one nature in the Word of God made flesh." On the strength of this purely verbal adhesion this Syrian Church is called monophysite, and specified as "Jacobite", after Jacob Baradai.[3]

Monophysite doctrine, claiming the support of St Cyril's name, was eagerly welcomed at Alexandria, where there was growing discontent with Byzantine administration[4] and the emperor's attempts to impose a patriarch of his own

[2] The heresy which is named after Nestorius, patriarch of Constantinople († c. 451), teaches that in our Lord there are two persons, God the Son and the man Jesus, and that Jesus alone was born of Mary and died on the cross. [*Trans.*]

[3] The heresy of Monophysism teaches that there is only one nature in Jesus Christ, his humanity being wholly absorbed in his divinity, and his body not of one substance with ours. [*Trans.*]—In the territory beyond the Euphrates formerly dependent on the Persian empire, the Jacobite patriarch of Antioch was represented by a delegate, the *mafrian*, who was looked on as on an equality with the Nestorian catholicos of Seleucia-Ctesiphon, later of Baghdad.

[4] Byzantine, i.e. appertaining to Byzantium, the old name of the city that had become Constantinople. [*Trans.*]

choosing. From 537 there was a monophysite Egyptian patriarch confronting the orthodox patriarch, and the newcomer soon had the support of practically all the Egyptian population, notably of its religious élite, the monks. The celebration of public worship in the Egyptian tongue (Coptic) was no doubt already traditional in the small towns and villages, and it was now introduced into the hellenized cities as a protest against the occupying Greek. This use of the local language as an outward sign of the constitution of a national Church soon spread to the patriarchate of Antioch, with Syriac[5]; this Aramaic dialect seems previously to have predominated only in East Syria, where the cultural centre of Edessa was adorned by the hymns and preaching of St Ephrem and the learning of the Persian school of theologians formed there in 363.

Armenia, which throughout the fifth century was struggling to throw off the Persian yoke, confirmed its ecclesiastical rupture at the Council of Valarshapat in 491; and in 506 the Council of Dvin solemnly condemned Chalcedon's teaching on Christ's two natures. Thus a third monophysite Church was constituted, and one bent even more than the others on differentiating its own rites and customs from those of Constantinople.

The Maronite Church

In the following century the efforts of the emperor Heraclius to find a compromise, one that would satisfy all parties in a divided Christendom, seems to have been the occasion of the formation of another independent Church. The monastery of St Maro, on the banks of the Orontes in Syria, suffered persecution from both orthodox Christians (Melkites) and from Jacobites; so the monks and their dependants—like so many others before and after them—sought refuge in the mountains of Lebanon. Whether or not they were at first

[5] Cf. C. Korolevsky, *Living Languages in Catholic Worship* (see Bibliography), pp. 6–7. [*Trans.*]

involved in Monothelitism—Heraclius's doctrine of one single will in Christ—these people developed into an autonomous Church during the eighth–ninth centuries; and they soon claimed to be the sole legitimate representatives of the old patriarchate of Antioch, that was now split into a Jacobite majority and an orthodox minority that was ever tightening its links with Constantinople. This, then, was the origin of the Maronite patriarchate of Antioch in Lebanon, which resisted the erosion caused by Islam better than any of its neighbouring Churches.

The Orthodox Churches

In face of all these secessions the communities that held to the faith of Chalcedon drew closer to Constantinople, and Christian orthodoxy began to be identified with loyalty to the empire: the name Melkite ("emperor's men"), given to Chalcedonians in the East and in Egypt, testified to this situation. There seem to have been very few Melkites in Egypt, but they were numerous in Syria, especially in the mountainous regions of Lebanon and the north; and the small patriarchate of Jerusalem was pretty solidly orthodox.

The numerous borrowings that the Great Church of the imperial capital made from Antiochene rites and usages facilitated the fusion that came about between the tenth and twelfth centuries. But long before that Justinian's legislation had given a common law to the orthodox Churches of the East, and this had a strong influence on the dissidents too. After the serious crises in the seventh century, the Council "in Trullo" in 692 succeeded in codifying the traditions of Eastern orthodoxy and fixing its institutions. The victory for orthodoxy in the iconoclast troubles of the eighth–ninth centuries put the final touch to this slow evolution, and assured the pre-eminence of the ecumenical patriarchate of Constantinople in Eastern orthodoxy.

The Christian East after Islam

At the time, then, that the Moslem conquests came to damp down its age-long fermentation, the Christian East had already attained the complex form that it still has. But in the course of time its different elements showed an unequal power of resistance in face of infidel domination. Only occasionally did the Arabs and Turks carry on violent persecution; but Christians were reduced to the status of second-class subjects, their vitality was gradually sapped, and the inducements of material prosperity and better treatment eventually brought about the apostasy of the majority of them.

The invaders were masters of the art of "dividing and ruling": they fomented and encouraged the antagonisms that had so long divided the Christian communities, and aggravated those doctrinal squabblings which were such a scandal, one that probably had contributed to the rise and spread of Islam. The Christian communities formed so many *millets*, "nations", the ecclesiastical head of each of which was responsible to the central authority for the collection of taxes and for everything that touched the personal standing of his people before the law: this system drove the Christian communities into a deeper and deeper isolation from one another. Nevertheless, they showed a fine vitality for a long time even after being cut off from the Byzantine empire, which lost more and more territory until it was finally extinguished by the capture of Constantinople by the Turks in 1453.

The Nestorian Church of Mesopotamia in particular had an astonishing history of missionary activity in central Asia and India. The Jacobites and, in a considerably lesser degree, the orthodox Melkites followed this example. The Coptic Church in Egypt continued to exercise an influence over the Ethiopian Church; and, thanks to the pilgrims and monks it sent to Jerusalem, the latter was also influenced by the Syrian Jacobites and even by the Armenians. As for orthodox Constantinople, she sent missionaries to evangelize the Russians and other Slav peoples, who were drawn into the orbit of her civilization, and often of her policies.

THE EASTERN CHURCHES TODAY

From the earliest moment that it had the opportunity, at the time of the Crusades, the Maronite Church has unbrokenly affirmed its communion with Rome and recognized the supreme jurisdiction of the see of Peter, the guardian of Catholic unity. With this exception, all the different Eastern Churches have at one time or another been separated from that communion. We have seen how this came about for the Nestorians and monophysites: it was a consequence of their refusal to accept the definitions made by the ecumenical councils of Ephesus or of Chalcedon. The Orthodox Churches are those that remained true to the faith of the first seven ecumenical councils, and these found themselves more and more drawn into the vicissitudes of the ecclesiastical relations between Old and New Rome. These relations were often broken off, in consequence of disagreements occasioned by very diverse factors. The best-known of these ruptures is that provoked by the election of Photius to the see of Constantinople in 858, an election judged by Rome to be uncanonical; and, even more, that brought about in 1054 when the legate of Pope St Leo IX, Cardinal Humbert of Moyenmoutier, formally excommunicated the patriarch Michael Cerularius. In spite of subsequent efforts to mend it, the break between Rome and Constantinople was irreparable after the Fourth Crusade of 1204, when the crusaders seized the imperial city and there set up by force an emperor and a patriarch imported from the Latin West.

On the other hand, the Crusades, and especially the activity of Franciscan and Dominican friars, prepared the way elsewhere for those reconciliations that led to the formation of Eastern Churches in renewed communion with Rome: among the Chaldeans (John Sulaqa in 1552), the Syrians (Andrew Akijian, 1662), the Melkites (Cyril Tanas, 1724), the Copts (Athanasius of Jerusalem, 1739), the Armenians (Abraham Ardzivian, 1740). Apart from these groups, some of them very small, which were found principally in Aleppo and Lebanon, there were two Catholic reunions on a large scale. On the Malabar coast of India (now Kerala), under the influence of the colonizing Portuguese, the reunion of the indigenous Christians of St Thomas, who were of Chaldean rite, was confirmed at the Synod of Diamper in 1599 (fifty years later many of them went into schism, and eventually put themselves under the Jacobite patriarch, exchanging their Chaldean rite for the West Syrian). At the same period several very important Orthodox dioceses in the then Polish Ukraine were reconciled with Rome, at the Synod of Brest-Litovsk in 1595; and in spite of serious difficulties and losses this Ruthenian[6] Church persisted as the largest body of Catholics of Byzantine rite. The second largest was formed by Rumanians in Transylvania, who were reconciled in 1697–1701. Since 1945 these two flourishing Churches, on the orders of communist governments, have been forcibly absorbed into the Orthodox patriarchates of Moscow and Rumania respectively.

The Churches that derive from the defections of the fifth century (sometimes called the Lesser Eastern Churches in English) are today mostly quite small bodies; but they are still important, because of the traditions that they represent, their great part in the early evangelization of Asia, and— what concerns us here—their liturgies of public worship, which illustrate cultures different from those of the Greek or Latin West.

The Armenians

Among these Churches, that of the Armenians has a place of its own. After fifteen centuries of tragic history, a history of invasion, massacre and migration, this people has remained faithful to the Christian faith and traditions which moulded the nation. A majority of them are still in their land of origin,

---

[6] "Ruthenian" is an ecclesiastical term for these (and some other) Byzantine-rite Catholics: ordinarily they are simply called Ukrainians. Subsequently to the Union of Brest their kinsmen in the Podkarpatska Rus ("Ruthenia") also reunited with Rome. [*Trans.*]

or have recently returned there; but there are large numbers of them settled in Europe and America, where they organize parishes where they are able (e.g. London, Manchester, New York). The Armenian Church is sometimes called "Gregorian", after St Gregory the Enlightener, the apostle of Armenia, and in principle it recognizes the supreme authority of the catholicos of Echmiadzin in the Armenian S.S.R. But in actuality this is a primacy of honour, and jurisdiction belongs in its own area to each of four sees: Echmiadzin, Sis in Cilicia (now at Antilyas in Lebanon), Jerusalem and Constantinople. The Catholic Armenians depend on the patriarch of Cilicia, whose see is now at Beirut, with residence at the monastery of Bzommar; the archbishopric of Lvov, for the Armenian colony in former Polish Galicia, was suppressed by the Russian government in 1946. In spite of these various jurisdictions and of religious and political disagreements, there is a fundamental solidarity among these dispersed people.

Latin influences have made their mark on the Armenian liturgy among the Catholics and, to a lesser but perceptible degree, among the dissidents too; but these infiltrations do not seriously affect the particular characteristics of a liturgy whose appointments and chants make it one of the most impressive in the East.

The Copts

While Armenians are to be found all over the globe, it is rare to meet Copts outside Egypt; they are peasants, deeply rooted in the banks of the Nile, and they do not often emigrate, in spite of their miserable poverty and the contempt sometimes shown for them by the large Moslem majority in the country. There are now only small clusters of them in the Delta, but they form compact groups in Upper Egypt, where they are free from outside influences. Egypt was the cradle of monasticism, and it has left a deep mark on the Coptic Church, in whose worship the ancient Egyptian language has been preserved (enriched by many words of Greek origin) as well as some melodies that may go back to the time of the Pharaohs. The austere archaism of this Church contrasts strongly with the liturgical splendours of the Greek, Syrian, Maronite and Armenian communities in the big towns of the Delta, notably Alexandria: this city is still what its founder, Alexander the Great, planned—a cosmopolitan centre, more Greek than Egyptian. There are still traces of the influence that the Syrian Jacobite Church exercised on its fellow monophysite Church of the Copts. For centuries Dair as-Suryani, "the Monastery of the Syrians", in the Nitrian desert, was one of the most flourishing intellectual centres of a Christian Egypt which, all too soon, was to sink into mediocrity; it is evidence of the solid faith of these humble *fellahin* that they survived it.

The Ethiopians

But the most notable achievement of the Coptic Church must be sought in Ethiopia (Abyssinia). Unanimous tradition gives the first place to Syrian missionaries in the evangelization of those people (probably originally from southern Arabia) who were under the rule of the princes of Axum. But from the first it was the patriarch of Alexandria who had supreme jurisdiction over the Ethiopian Christians: it was he who appointed an Egyptian monk to be their bishop, the only one authorized to ordain clergy for them (this hierarch was called *abuna*, "our father"). The new empire of Ethiopia, that from the thirteenth century grew up in the high lands of Tigrai, Lasta and Shoa, was still more religiously dependent on the Coptic Church, which was then reorganizing itself and throwing off Syrian influence. Ethiopia's successful resistance to Islam in the middle of the sixteenth century was made possible by Portuguese help; but the ecclesiastical and other blunders of their Western allies were such that the oldest and most important Christian nation in Africa shut itself up in an almost complete isolation, and so remained until recent years.

When control by the Egyptian Church was reduced simply to the material intermediaryship of *abuna*, the Ethiopian Church gave rein to an enthusiastic and fanciful piety, nourished on judaizing and apocalyptical legends, that was very different from Coptic austerity. Its peculiar situation, its numerical importance and its ancient tradition should give the Ethiopian Church a special place in the emergence of a Christian Africa that is conscious of its differences from Europe; but for that it must have a clergy alive to the new needs and conditions of Christian life. The Greek Orthodox Churches have grasped the position, and, ignoring age-old disputes, do not hesitate to treat as Orthodox a Church that still clings obstinately to monophysite formulas. Every facility has been given to Ethiopian students to study theology at Athens and at the patriarchal college of Halki in Turkey; and the organizers of the Coptic Institute at Cairo, concerned to keep the traditional religious bonds between the Christians of Egypt and those of Ethiopia, are interested in these students too.

Catholics of Ethiopian rite are still few; but being in close touch with the world-wide Catholic Church they can greatly help their country to accept the wider vocation that is now open to it, without forsaking anything of its own tradition. Ethiopia has, in circumstances of great difficulty, kept the treasure received from its first apostles, developed it in her own way, and assimilated elements from all parts of the Christian world: she is well-placed to take on new responsibilities.

The Syrian Jacobites

There is a similar opportunity for Churches of the Syrian tradition, through their daughter Churches in southern India. After a fine record of religion and learning up to the thirteenth century, the Syrian Jacobites, so eaten away by Islam, are now relatively few; so too are the Catholics of Syrian rite: but both these Churches have an *élite* of clergy and laity

able to profit by their heritage. In India, the Malabar Jacobites, chance fruit of sad events, have since 1930 experienced
a promising movement towards reintegration into Catholic
communion. Today, the followers of the late Mar Ivanios,
the Catholic Malankarese, are relatively the most prolific in
vocations to the priesthood of any Church in India, and full
of enthusiasm to bring the Gospel to non-Christians.

The Nestorian Church

These unexpected transplantations and developments
among a people and culture so different from those of Syria
and Mesopotamia are no less remarkable when we turn to
the East Syrians or Chaldeans, whose early history we have
already seen. In the twelfth and thirteenth centuries the Nestorian Church numbered millions of people, in 27 provinces
and 200 dioceses, all across Asia to India and China. Today
there remain but two insignificant groups: one, the Nestorian
Church proper, after being isolated in the mountains of
Kurdistan, was decimated by massacre, and lost its catholicos,
who in 1933 sought refuge in the United States; the other is
a mere handful of people in Malabar, resulting from a nine-
teenth-century schism from the Catholic Church. The Malabar union brought about by the Portuguese in 1599 was
accompanied by a deplorable westernization of the Indians'
organization and Chaldean rite, which led to the schism in
1653. Accordingly, the Catholic Syro-Malabar Church, which
represents a very large proportion of the Catholic population
of India, has a very hybrid appearance; but at the present
time, encouraged by Rome, it is seeking to recover all that
was good in its original traditions, and with it the influence
that such an old and perfectly Indian Church deserves to have.

The Maronite Church

The Maronite Church is another heir to the traditions of the
Church of Antioch, having a twofold descent, Aramaean and
Hellenic, and in a certain way it is a bridge-church between

East and West. Its determination to emphasize its indefectible Catholicity and faithfulness to the Roman see has led it to adopt in public worship many external usages of the Roman rite, and these disguise its authentic liturgical tradition; but it has lovingly treasured the essentials of the Syrian Christian tradition, which it has done more than any other Church to keep alive. This tradition has been expounded to the world by Maronite scholars (notably the four Assemani) and by the presence of those others who, pushing ever further along the routes opened by their Phoenician ancestors, have carried an image of Christian Lebanon all over the world. This Church had its origin in a monastery, and its monks, sooner and more generally than elsewhere, adapted themselves to apostolic and missionary work: monasticism has put a permanent stamp on the Maronite Church but, unlike some others, without shutting it up in a religiousness too exclusively concerned with "the last things". The Lebanese is enterprising and adventurous, and in his ancestral faith he finds a reliable support that enables him actively to cope with new situations without losing his soul in the process.

The Churches of Byzantine rite

It is out of the question to give a sketch in a few lines of the characteristic features of the Churches of Byzantine rite, daughters of the Church of Constantinople or formed in that pattern. In any case a volume in this series will be devoted to them, and so it is sufficient here to indicate their geographical distribution. First of all there must be mentioned those Churches that represent the remnants in the patriarchates of Alexandria and Antioch of those who were faithful to Chalcedonian orthodoxy, and the patriarchate of Jerusalem—the people called Melkites. They were made up principally of families which, because of their descent or form of culture, were moved to cling to Greek tradition and to the Byzantine empire that represented it; they were vexatiously treated by the dissidents, who stirred up the Moslems against them. But a sharp distinction must be made between the Orthodox patriarchates of Antioch and of Alexandria: the Antiochene faithful are solidly established, especially in the Orontes valley and Lebanon; but in the Alexandrian patriarchate they are a minority made up mostly of Greek immigrants, prone to identify Orthodoxy with the Hellenism to which they are fanatically devoted. The Christians of Palestine ceased to speak Syriac and became arabized long ago: but the Orthodox Patriarch of Jerusalem is still a Greek, and he rules with the support of the monastic Brotherhood of the Holy Sepulchre ("Hagiotaphites"), the guardian of Hellenic Orthodoxy in the Holy Places.

In the seventeenth and eighteenth centuries a movement towards Rome developed among the Melkites, notably at Aleppo and in southern Lebanon; and when the patriarchs Cyril V († 1720) and, particularly, Cyril VI Tanas (†1760) had declared their communion with Rome a Catholic Melkite patriarchate was organized. In 1772 the patriarch was given jurisdiction as well over Byzantine Catholics in Palestine and Egypt, who were mostly emigrants from Syria and Lebanon.[7]

After the events of 1204 the patriarchate of Constantinople remained outside Catholic communion, the reunions at the Councils of Lyons (1274) and Florence (1439) coming to nothing. His Church reduced by the constitution of autocephalous Churches over which he has only a primacy of honour, the Ecumenical Patriarch today exercises effective jurisdiction only over the Orthodox of Turkey and the Dodekanese and the Greeks dispersed under local hierarchs in western Europe, the Americas and elsewhere, with some rights in Crete.

The Church of Greece gained self-government in 1833, and is organized on a synodal basis, the archbishop of Athens

---

[7] The title of the Catholic Melkite patriarch is "Patriarch of Antioch and all the East, Alexandria and Jerusalem". Hierarchically he is the most important of the Eastern Catholic bishops.—The liturgical language of the two Byzantine patriarchates of Antioch is now Arabic (formerly Greek and Syriac.) [Trans.]

being president of the synod. The Church of Cyprus is considered of apostolic foundation because the island was first evangelized by St Barnabas, and it has been autocephalous for fifteen hundred years. These three Churches—Constantinople, Greece, Cyprus—are purely Hellenic and use only Greek in public worship.

The local language was adopted sooner or later in those Orthodox Churches that were organized among the Slavs and Rumanians. The earliest of these was that of the Bulgars, whose archbishop received the title of patriarch from the pope in 927; since 1953 Bulgaria has again been a patriarchate. Then came the Church of the principality of Kiev (Russia) in the eleventh century. Both these Churches soon translated the Byzantine liturgy into Old Bulgarian or Slavonic, which the invention of the Cyrillic alphabet had made the first written Slav language. Through their association with Constantinople, these Churches eventually found themselves separated from Catholic communion. It was the same with the Church of Serbia, which first became a patriarchate in 1346, in the reign of the great Stephen III Dushan; the Serbian patriarchate was revived in 1922.

The metropolitan of Kiev having subscribed to union with Rome at the Council of Florence, a dissident metropolitan was appointed at Moscow in 1448; and in 1492 the metropolitan Zossima publicly declared that, Constantinople having fallen into the hands of the Turks, Moscow had inherited its place and become the Third Rome. A century later this claim was underwritten ecclesiastically and Moscow became a patriarchal see.

The Orthodox of Rumania depended first on the Bulgarian Church and then on that of Constantinople, and did not form a self-governing Church till 1885. They then followed the example of their countrymen of Transylvania in the liturgical use of the Rumanian language. After the first world war all Rumanians were united into one state, and in 1925 a patriarchate of Rumania was set up for the first time.

CHAPTER II

WHAT IS A RITE?

So far we have been concerned with Churches. As a matter
of history, the Christian East differed from the Christian West
in that it was organized in a number of bodies that were
autonomous in relation to one another, though in communion
with one another and with the Apostolic See of Rome, cus-
todian of that unity. This communion in the faith and the
sacraments of the faith left a very large field of free choice
in matters of spiritual life and church discipline. The essential
lines of this discipline were laid down by the fourth-century
councils that fixed the formulation of religious faith, and their
decisions were universally accepted as the basis of ecclesiastical or canon law. Little by little the framework was filled in,
completed and applied by the canonical enactments, "canons",
of local councils or the decrees of patriarchs that carried the
requisite authority. The consequent variousness of discipline
sometimes had an adverse effect on the relations between the
different Churches, and not infrequently led to or aggravated
disputes. The Trullan or "Quinisext" council of 692, which
legislated for the orthodox patriarchates of Constantinople,
Alexandria and Antioch, sought to give its discipline something of the weight of doctrinal orthodoxy, though that discipline differed on several points from that of the West; the
popes, conscious of the legitimacy of Western customs,
challenged this "tie-up", and the affair helped to strengthen
the growing distrust between the Greek and Roman churches.
Such regrettable things might have been avoided had both

sides had a more acute consciousness of the inevitable element
of contingency in disciplinary decisions, which have to take
account of an actual situation in which place, time and social
background are factors.

The whole body of its ecclesiastical institutions is the
expression of a Church's concrete reality, the product of a
civilization, as well as of its original transcendent impulse
nourished by the study of the Bible and by the living apostolic
tradition. And he who understands such institutions from
inside can grasp the very mystery of the Church, herself caught
up in that process of incarnation by means of which God's
pattern of salvation is worked out. From the second century
onwards the Church defined herself as catholic, universal, in
distinction from every sect or party, thus emphasizing that in
her, and in her alone, every man and every human society
can realize their deepest and finest ambitions. This univer-
sality naturally finds expression in the diversity of customs
and observances proper to each local tradition within the one
religious fellowship, which itself finds its expression in
institutions.

The see of Rome, founded by St Peter, realized more and
more clearly as time went by that it was heir to the promises
made to Peter: that it was by divine appointment guardian of
unity in the faith and of fellowship in charity, and that therefore it had the final word in deciding the degree to which
the customs of each local Church were compatible with the
maintenance of a universal unity. It is alas! only too true
that from time to time, at moments of crisis or through insuf-
ficient knowledge of local conditions, the West has shown
itself too fond of a legalistic uniformity, and has not given
enough respect to legitimate local tradition. But it must be
said that the more regrettable examples of this were often
the work of subordinate authorities—when they were not due
to the civil power or to missionary clergy acting "on their
own". For centuries the Christians of East and West were
almost totally ignorant of one another; separated communi-

ties, often encouraged by their Moslem masters, nursed old grudges and peevishly kept themselves to themselves: a state of affairs like that made it almost impossible to appreciate a different tradition and see that it was complementary to one's own. The "latinizing" measures that found favour in Rome from the twelfth to the nineteenth centuries (Dom Guéranger seems to have been their last notable defender) find parallels in the great Byzantine canonist Theodore Balsamon († *c.* 1196), in his contemporary the Jacobite patriarch Michael the Great, and in sundry other Eastern canonists who followed them.

Indeed, the popes of Rome were perhaps the first and warmest defenders of local particularities. Leo XIII's constitution *Orientalium dignitas* (1894) is a charter whose force is not exhausted. It looks back to the famous *Etsi pastoralis* (1742) of that great canonist Benedict XIV, and forward to the teaching of the twentieth-century popes, which is perhaps best summed up in Pius XII's encyclical letter *Orientalis ecclesiae decus*, for the fifteenth centenary of St Cyril of Alexandria (1944):

> Each and every people of Eastern rite must have its rightful freedom in all that is bound up with its own history and with its own genius and character, saving always the truth and integrity of the teaching of Jesus Christ. . . . Everyone must be fully assured that they will never have to give up their own legitimate rites and ancient institutions for Latin rites and institutions. All these are to be held in equal esteem and honour, for they adorn the Church, our common mother, as with a queenly garment. This diversity of rites and institutions, and the safeguarding of what is old and precious in each, does not at all stand in the way of true and genuine unity.

There have been many attempts to minimize Leo XIII's provisions, and in the above document Pius XII cuts these attempts short with careful precision. He makes it clear that the term "rite" covers not only the outward aspects of the

Church's prayer and organization—gestures, vestments and insignia, regulations: it includes also everything "to do with the sacred liturgy and the hierarchical Orders and with the other aspects of Christian life". This is an extremely wide interpretation of "rite", but it is in fact the only one that expresses what the word has always meant to the Eastern Churches.

Nor is it an arbitrary interpretation. It took the sad decay of liturgical life in the West since the later Middle Ages, the neglect of the sacramental significance of each Christian celebration, its visible, ritual, expression of the mystery of the Church, it took this to give "rite" the narrow meaning with which we are familiar. Such a thing could not happen in Churches whose particular grace seems to have been intensively to live the liturgical mystery as the highest and best expression of the mystery of salvation, and to do this in the darkest and most degenerate times. The mystery of salvation, that is, God's hidden purpose made manifest in Christ's redeeming work, finds its fulfilment in this world in that Passover observance to which our Lord gave its full meaning when he linked it with his passion and resurrection, those acts by which he associated mankind with his triumph over death and enabled us to pass to the Father with him. The Eucharist, in memory of him, is the heart and peak of Christian worship: it shows forth the definitive gathering of saved mankind around the messianic table, and in mystery brings that gathering about.

The full meaning of "rite" is clear enough to anyone who understands what the Church's liturgy is and what man is— a created being who is both body and soul, who normally finds his fullest opportunities only in the company of his fellows, who belongs to a tradition and is dependent on a whole geographical and historical environment which finds expression in a culture. The inescapable consequence is that, as Pius XII declared, every aspect and institution of Christian life is inseparably involved in the idea of "rite". The Churches of the East have been shaped by a long history, by a common destiny of very special conditions, that were often hard and sometimes called for heroism. The liturgy is simply the highest and most perfect way in which these Churches show us their true countenance and, behind it, their soul. It cannot be isolated or torn from its living setting. Its liturgy of worship is the sacred expression of a human community at the moment when Christ enables it to join in the priestly action by which he takes mankind with him to the Father.

But the human race is not just a collection of disembodied individuals: it is made up of communities brought together by a common destiny. Man transforms the community, which becomes conditioned by a religious outlook, by a theology, by customs sanctioned by law. And so, today as in the past, a local Church is a cell of the world-wide Catholic Church, and is called to make its own voice heard in that great fellowship. Every considerable culture is invited to expand and excel itself in a liturgy, in institutions and ways of Christian living, that are particular expressions of the common faith. The whole West has been formed by Latin *romanitas*, modified in this place and that by a particular temperament; the Eastern Churches, heirs and living witnesses to other great civilizations, are a significant lesson for the young Churches now growing up in Africa and Asia.

CHAPTER III

THE LITURGICAL
FAMILIES OF THE EAST

The Westerner who is present at different Eastern liturgies is soon struck by certain common characteristics which differentiate them from the Latin liturgy: for example, the solemnity of the celebration, which is always sung[1]; the presence of an altar screen, whether or not covered with icons, or (as with the Armenians) of a veil with which the altar can be screened[2]; the important part taken by the deacon. Other unfamiliar usages are proper to particular Churches, such as the solemn bringing of the bread and wine to the altar, while the *Cherubikon* is sung, in Byzantine churches. Going beyond such external matters (which are sometimes of minor importance), it is not too difficult to distinguish between (1) the Churches of Syriac language, more or less direct successors of the old patriarchate of Antioch, namely, Syrian (Jacobite or Catholic), Maronite, and Syro-Indian (Jacobite or Catholic); East Syrian (Nestorian or Chaldean Catholic),[3] Syro-Malabar (Catholic); (2) the Churches of Byzantine rite (Greek, Melkite, Russian, Ruthenian Catholic, Rumanian, Bulgarian, Serbian, etc.), and the Armenian Churches (dissident or Catholic), whose liturgy has many points in common with the

[1] In recent times Catholics of some Eastern rites have introduced "low Mass", in imitation of the West and in flat contradiction of unanimous Eastern tradition.

[2] The use of a veil has been given up by the Maronites, under Western influence.

[3] In this book the terms "East Syrian" and "Chaldean" are sometimes used interchangeably, though it is usual to reserve the second for the Chaldean Catholics of Iraq.

Byzantine; and (3) the Coptic and Ethiopian Churches, dissident or Catholic.

A closer examination in relation to ancient sources enables us to distinguish two great liturgical families, respectively Antiochene and Alexandrian, the latter having certain points of resemblance to the Roman liturgy. The liturgies of Jerusalem and the Churches of Asia Minor have disappeared, but they had considerable influence on the Byzantine and Armenian rites.

The differences between the rites of the largely hellenized West Syria (Antioch) and those of East Syria (Mesopotamia) probably go back ultimately to the twofold movement of evangelization that can be detected in apostolic times: one, dominated by St Paul, was addressed directly to more or less hellenized pagans; the other sought to proclaim the Gospel to Jewish communities and was largely based on their religious and liturgical traditions.

ORIGINS (SECOND–FIFTH CENTURIES)

There is a valuable document which tells us about the organization and liturgical life of the Church towards the middle of the third century in a Greek-speaking Syrian community that was strongly marked by Jewish tradition. A century and a half later this *Didascalia Apostolorum* (Doctrine of the Apostles) formed the basis of an enlarged work, the first six books of the *Apostolic Constitutions*.[4] What these tell us can be completed from more certain sources: the "mystagogical catecheses" on Christian initiation and the eucharistic celebration given at Antioch after 381 by Theodore of Mopsuestia, catecheses by St John Chrysostom († 407) and sermons of his at Antioch and Constantinople, catecheses by St Cyril of Jerusalem († 386) or his successor John, the diary of a pilgrimage to the Near East at the end of the fourth

---

[4] Trans. of the *Didascalia Apostolorum* by R. H. Connolly (Oxford, 1929); of the *Constitutiones Apostolorum* by J. Donaldson in Ante-Nicene Christian Library XVII (Edinburgh, 1870), pt 2.

century by a nun named Etheria, who came from Spain or southern Gaul.[5] In addition to these rich sources, attempts have been made at reconstruction on the basis of later liturgical books. Books vii and viii of the *Apostolic Constitutions* already contain two interesting sets of liturgical prayers. Book vii is largely adapted from a work in Greek attributed to Hippolytus of Rome, called the *Apostolic Tradition*, written between the years 200 and 215 and resembling the Syrian *Didascalia*. The original has been lost, but it has been reconstructed by an English scholar, Dom R. H. Connolly, with the help of an incomplete Latin translation and of adaptations which were particularly widely spread in the Church of Alexandria. Another adaptation, included in a fifth-century Syrian apocryphal writing, the *Testamentum Domini*, contains liturgical texts that are still in use in the Syrian rite.[6]

On a basis of later versions it has even been possible to reconstruct with considerable likelihood the original form of the anaphora (eucharistic prayer, "canon of the Mass") as it was at Antioch and in East Syria, which was dominated by the cultural influence of Edessa during the third and fourth centuries. Here are these two prayers and, what is perhaps still older, that in the *Apostolic Tradition*; this last continued to be used so far from its land of origin as Ethiopia.

Antiochene anaphora[7]

It is fitting and right to glorify you, to worship you, to give you thanks, you who indeed are God (with your Son and

[5] Theodore, tr. by A. Mingana in Woodbrooke Studies, no. vi (1933); Chrysostom, French tr. by A. Wenger, *Huit Catéchèses . . .* (Paris, 1957), and his sermons *passim* (Eng. tr. in the Library of the Fathers); Cyril, tr. by F. L. Cross (London, 1951); Etheria, tr. by M. L. McLure and C. L. Feltoe (London, 1921).

[6] *The Apostolic Tradition*, tr. B. S. Easton (Cambridge, 1934); *The Testament of Our Lord*, tr. J. Cooper and A. J. McLean (Edinburgh, 1902).

[7] Reconstructed by A. Raes: "L'authenticité de la liturgie byzantine de S. Jean Chrysostome" (*Orientalia christiana periodica*, XXIV, 1–2, pp. 5–16; Rome, 1958). The passages in brackets seem not to have formed part of the primitive version.

your Holy Spirit). It is you who brought us into existence out of nothingness; and after we had fallen you raised us up, and left nothing undone that we might be brought back to Heaven and receive your gift of the kingdom that is to come.

We thank you for all these things (with your only-begotten Son and your Holy Spirit). (Cherubim and six-winged seraphim stand before you, shouting with loud voice and saying: Holy, holy, holy. . . .)

(You are holy, all holy, you and your only-begotten Son and your Holy Spirit.) You are holy, all holy, your glory is sublime. You so loved the world that you gave it your only-begotten Son that all those who believe in him should not perish but should have everlasting life. After he had come and had fulfilled his whole design (*oikonomia*) towards us, in the night that he was betrayed he took bread in his hands, and blessed it and gave it to his followers the apostles, saying: Take, eat; this is my body which is broken for you for forgiveness of sins. In the same way with the cup, after they had supped, saying: Drink, all of you, of it; this is the blood of the new covenant, shed for you and for the multitude for forgiveness of sins. So, Lord, calling to mind this command of the Saviour and all that he did for us, the cross, the resurrection on the third day, the going up into the heavens, the sitting at the right hand and the second coming in glory, we glorify you for all and for everything, we bless you and we pray you, Lord, to send your Holy Spirit on these offerings (make this bread the worshipful body of Christ and this cup the blood of Christ) that they may be forgiveness of sins to those that receive them (imparting of the Holy Spirit for the fullness of the kingdom, and confidence before you).

Chaldean anaphora of the Apostles[8]

It is fitting that every mouth should glorify, every voice confess, every creature revere and proclaim the worshipful and glorious Name (of the all-holy Trinity of the Father, of the Son and of the Holy Spirit) who created the world in his grace and its inhabitants in his goodness, who saved mankind in his

[8] Reconstructed by B. Botte: "L'anaphore chaldéenne des Apôtres" (*Orientalia christiana periodica*, xv, 3–4, pp. 259–276; Rome, 1949).

mercy and bestowed an immense boon on mortal human-
kind. . . .

We your servants confess you, Lord, for you have conferred
so great a grace on us that we can make no recompense. You
took on our manhood, you came down in your godhead, you
raised our lowliness, mended our rottenness, revived our mortal
flesh, forgave our transgressions, made good our sins, en-
lightened our understanding, overcame our enemies, gave
honour to our littleness. We respond to the superabundance of
your grace, O Lord our God, with hymns, with praise, with
acknowledgement and with worship, now and always, and for
ever and ever. Amen. [The recital of the institution is not
reproduced; cf. page 90.]

We too, Lord, your servants, gathered together in your
name now stand before you, we to whom the Mystery that
comes from you has been handed down. Joyfully we glorify
and exalt, we commemorate and we carry out this great, awe-
some, holy, divine mystery of the passion, death, burial and
resurrection of our Lord and Saviour Jesus Christ. And for
the great, the immense and wonderful, work (*oikonomia*) that
has been done amongst us, we, full-throatedly and with face
unveiled, give thanks to you and ceaselessly praise you in the
Church that is ransomed by the precious blood of your Christ.
We respond with hymns, with praise, with acknowledgement
and with worship to your holy, life-giving, living name, now
and always and for ever and ever. Amen.

Anaphora of the Apostolic Tradition of Hippolytus[9]

We give you thanks, O God, through your beloved servant
Jesus Christ, whom in these last times you sent to us as saviour
and redeemer and messenger of your will. He is your insepar-
able Word, through him you created all things, and in him
you were well-pleased. You sent him from Heaven into a
virgin's womb, within her he was made flesh, and was manifested as your Son, born of the Holy Spirit and the Virgin.

[9] From the Latin text in R. H. Connolly's *The So-called Egyptian
Church Order* (Cambridge, 1916), p. 176. The whole document is
translated by B. S. Easton in *The Apostolic Tradition of Hippolytus*
(Cambridge, 1934), pp. 33–61.

Fulfilling your will and gathering a people holy to you, he stretched forth his hands in his passion that he might set free from suffering those who have believed in you.

When he was betrayed to suffering which he freely accepted that he might overcome death, and break Satan's bonds, and tread Hell underfoot, and give light to holy ones, and establish the covenant and show forth the resurrection, he took bread and gave thanks to you and said: Take, eat: this is my body, which will be broken for you. The same with the cup, saying: This is my blood, which is shed for you. Whenever you do this, do it in memory of me.

Therefore, calling to mind his death and resurrection, we offer you the bread and the cup, giving you thanks because you have counted us worthy to stand before you and to serve you. And we pray you to send your Holy Spirit upon the holy Church's offering; to gather into one all the holy people who partake, to fill them with the Holy Spirit that their faith may be confirmed in the truth, and that thus we may praise and glorify you through your servant Jesus Christ. Through him be glory and honour to you, the Father and the Son with the Holy Spirit in your holy Church, now and for ever and ever. Amen.

These three prayers may be considered to antedate the theological and liturgical developments of the fourth century, and differences of temperament are already clear in them, even allowing for the first two being partly conjectural reconstructions and the third the work of a teacher whose influence on its original thought appears here and there. Nor must it be forgotten that at that time there were doubtless no formulas fixed once for all, but that each celebrant developed a traditional pattern in his own way. Having said that, the lack of doctrinal explicitness must be noticed in the East Syrian anaphora, and also that its expression is characteristically semitic. The Antiochene anaphora stresses the economy of salvation, the looking forward to the end of time, and the splendour of God's glory, and these characteristics persisted in the Syrian rite. The anaphora of Hippolytus is characterized by the importance given to the mission of the Word—a doctrine specially dear to Hippolytus—and also by its sobriety and sense of the Church. These aspects are found again in the later anaphoras of the Roman and Alexandrian rites.

For Alexandria we have no documents comparable with those available for the Syrian rites. The Egyptian teachers were concerned above all with spiritual life and gave little attention to external observances: no baptismal catechesis has survived and, if it had, it is a matter for speculation whether it would have given us any exact information about the conduct of public worship. On the other hand, we are lucky to have a euchology, a collection of liturgical prayers for the use of a bishop celebrant, attributed to a friend of St Athanasius, St Serapion of Thmuis who died *c*. 360. An eleventh-century copy of this was found among the manuscripts on Mount Athos in 1894. If this document as we have it includes some later elements, it still enables us to see the main lines of the baptismal and eucharistic services in Egypt at the middle of the fourth century. As with Hippolytus, it is a matter of a personal collection, made by a bishop theologian who wanted to integrate into the liturgy the doctrinal developments called for by the preoccupations of his day, and it bears the mark of the compiler. In those formative times, before formulas were fixed by long tradition, it was easier to express the Church's living faith in liturgical prayers, and thus to forearm the faithful against the dangers of error arising from Trinitarian and Christological controversies. The Eastern liturgies are always didactic, notably the Byzantine, which has made particularly good use of this line of development.

THE DEVELOPED FORMS

Between the fifth and the tenth centuries liturgies in the East, as in the West, attained their definitive forms, and subsequent developments and alterations only rarely involved any substantial change. It is not possible here to follow the development of each of them, and in any case for most of them the state of historical research does not permit of such an examination. Particularly for the East Syrian and Coptic rites, the available texts are practically all very late; the surviving commentaries are very few, and mostly still unpublished, and the information to be gleaned from religious or secular writers, especially historians and hagiographers, have not yet been brought together. Even in the case of the Antiochene and Byzantine rites, which are the best known, there are no really critical editions, still less comparative editions, and these are necessary bases for any serious historical study. So far, each individual researcher—and they are few—has had to make his own collection of accessible material, and such collections are inevitably fragmentary. Only an historical and comparative study, grounded on incontestable foundations, can be really explanatory. Without that, we have to stop short at a simply external description, which does not allow us to penetrate to the inner significance of this or that rite or to set out the different interpretations given it in course of time, often for non-essential reasons. This makes it very difficult to attain the main object of liturgical science, which is to meet the living soul of a community as it expresses itself in its official religious celebrations. So we have to be content here with a few short notes on each of the actually existing rites.

THE SYRIAN LITURGICAL FAMILY: THE EAST SYRIAN BRANCH

The Syro-Mesopotamian rites, Nestorian and Chaldean

There are several reasons for beginning this study with the East Syrian or Mesopotamian rites, which seem at an early date to have been given their characteristic features in the Church of Edessa, that influential spiritual and intellectual home of Syriac speech and semitic culture. The regions of the Euphrates and the Tigris were evangelized mainly from

Antioch; but these provinces were little affected by Hellenism, they spoke Aramaic dialects, and their Jewish communities, numerous since the Babylonian exile, were reinforced by new and active elements after Jerusalem was destroyed by Titus and the Jews dispersed: and it certainly seems that Christianity there, more than anywhere else, kept the semitic traits of the first Jewish Churches. This requires that special attention be given to the tradition of the East Syrian Churches, in these times of ours when there is again a problem of the expression of the Christian faith and life in cultures that are conscious of their different origins from those of the Greco-Roman world.

Edessa appears to have had a particularly important part in the development of the writing and use of hymns among Christians. The oldest known hymns, the *Odes of Solomon*, without doubt belong to northern Syria or Asia Minor; but towards the end of the second century Bardesanes of Edessa wrote 150 hymns, unorthodox in tone, which became so popular that, in the middle of the fourth century, St Ephrem borrowed their rhythms and tunes and set them to orthodox words: this was the beginning of a hymnody common to all the Syriac-speaking Churches, and its influence was felt throughout Christendom.

But apart from these hymns little is known of the ancient liturgy of Edessa, which soon spread to Persia, Armenia and India.[10] After the Romano-Persian wars at the time of Heraclius, and the Arab conquest, the Nestorian Church underwent a reorganization accompanied by liturgical codification. This extended from the time of the catholicos Ishu'yab III (650–658), to whom is ascribed the putting into order of the *Hudra*, the book of the Divine Office for Sundays, feasts of our Lord

[10] The Council of Seleucia in 410 decided to conform the doctrine and discipline of the Chaldean Church to those of its western neighbours. No doubt it was then that it introduced such usages as the anaphora of the Apostles, from the Antioch region, and of that called "of Theodore of Mopsuestia", which may have been an adaptation of a liturgy from Asia Minor.

and during the "fast of Nineveh", to Yaballaha II (1190–1222), who gave its final form to the *Gazza*, the collection of hymns, antiphons, prayers and homilies for all feasts of the year. Yaballaha's predecessor, Elias III abu-Halim (1176–90), had added to the psalter prayers composed by himself or taken from ancient authors. From at least the seventh century there were used, besides the old anaphora of the Apostles, two other anaphoras, imported from Antioch but remodelled to accord with East Syrian tradition: these were given the names of Theodore of Mopsuestia, "the Interpreter" (of the Scriptures) and of Nestorius himself. The services of baptism and ordination are supposed to have been fixed by Ishu'yab III. The Ordinary (*Typikon*) of the Upper Monastery (Dayra 'Ellayta) at Mosul played a most important part in settling the organization of the Mesopotamian liturgy.

Since their union with Rome in 1552 the Catholic Chaldeans have adopted a number of usages of the Western Church: forms for the sacraments of penance and of anointing the sick (not found in the Nestorian books) have been taken over, together with certain feasts, prayers and devotional practices. At the present time their liturgical books are undergoing revision to get rid of unfortunate hybridisms and to restore purity of tradition, while taking account of adaptations that are legitimate.

The Syro-Malabar rite

When the Portuguese came into contact with the Christians of the south-west coast of India these were using, as from time immemorial, the liturgy of Mesopotamia, doubtless with some peculiarities of their own. Unhappily, the ancient books were destroyed after the Synods of Goa (1585) and Diamper (1599), which imposed the use of many Western rites and formulas, translated into Syriac; some of these were taken from the books of Braga and Coïmbra. The liturgy has been celebrated in this hybrid form by the Catholic Syro-Malabarese down to our own day.

THE SYRIAN LITURGICAL FAMILY: THE WEST SYRIAN BRANCH

The Antiochene rite among Jacobites and Catholics

Something is known of the oldest liturgy of Antioch thanks to the *Didascalia Apostolorum* (see page 36). From the fourth century several usages were imported from Jerusalem, notably the eucharistic anaphora called "of St James", and from then on the Antiochene liturgy was characterized by much splendour and by the place it gave to non-biblical hymns. St John Chrysostom's homilies and other sources testify to the enthusiasm of the people of Antioch for processions, especially for those held at night; vigils seem to have been exceptionally in favour. Early in the sixth century the patriarch Severus, the great doctor of the monophysites, compiled a collection of chants, a sort of antiphoner, arranged according to the liturgical cycle and the order of services; this was known as the *Oktoekhos*, and in the following century it was translated into Syriac by James of Edessa. Meanwhile the formal rupture of the monophysites with Constantinople had resulted in the Jacobite Church constructing a liturgy in Syriac. This, side by side with purely Antiochene elements translated from Greek, appears to have drawn largely on customs of communities which had always used their native Syriac, as well as on the rich resources provided at Edessa by St Ephrem and his followers. In spite of the radical and often violent opposition between the Jacobite Church and the Nestorian Church, these borrowings—sometimes on a basis of tit for tat —seem to have gone on for a long time.

In its main parts the work of the great Jacobite doctors and patriarchs of the seventh and eighth centuries, this liturgy long remained open to new compositions, not only as regards hymns, which have a place in it not equalled elsewhere, but also for such important things as eucharistic anaphoras and the rites of baptism and penance. Definitive codification came only in the second half of the twelfth century, with Dionysius bar Salibi and his contemporary the patriarch Michael the Great, to whom the Antiochene Pontifical is owed. But some of the seventy-two anaphoras that still exist are later. All through this period the Jacobite liturgy went on adopting Byzantine customs, whether by direct contact after the empire reconquered Syria in 968, or through Jerusalem, whose liturgy was more and more closely connected with that of the imperial capital.

For the Syrians, as for the Chaldeans, union with Rome brought a certain westernization in the ministering of the sacraments; but the Latin usages confirmed by the Council of Sharfeh in 1888 were but few, so that the original purity of the Antiochene rite is safeguarded. It was imported into India by the dissidents after the Malabar schism of 1653 and translated into Malayalam, the local language: it is celebrated there today in this tongue both by the Malabar Jacobites and by the small minority of Catholic Malankarese.

The Maronite rite

The migration of the monastery of St Maro from the banks of the Orontes to the mountains and deep valleys of northern Lebanon (cf. pages 18–19) gave rise to a new version of the Antiochene rite, with features of its own. Little is known of its early history, before the Maronites came into direct relations with Rome through the twelfth-century crusaders; but after that it was subject to Latin influence of an intensity unequalled in any other Eastern Church.[11] This began very early in the thirteenth century, when Maronite bishops took to using Western insignia, and was strengthened in the sixteenth and seventeenth centuries under the influence of Franciscan and Jesuit missioners. The patriarch Stephen Duaihi (1670–1704) undertook the preparation of an edition of the Ritual

[11] Except perhaps in some respects the Syro-Malabarese since the sixteenth century. In either case the appearance of westernization is accentuated by the amount of it that affects externals, vestments, arrangement of churches, and so on. [Trans.]

and the Pontifical; but unhappily, both at the Council of Luwayzeh in 1736 and later, the supporters of latinization carried the day, and it was not till 1942 that the Maronite Church had a Ritual that conformed to its own old tradition.

The eucharistic liturgy and the daily office have been changed less; they are celebrated in accordance with the old rite of Antioch, with certain noticeable peculiarities whose origins appear to go back a very long way. For instance, one of the seven anaphoras preserved in the Maronite rite is an archaic composition which has some analogy with the ancient anaphora of the Apostles.

THE SYRO-ASIAN BRANCH

The Byzantine liturgies

In spite of the considerable influence of Cappadocian and Pontic customs, and more generally of those of all the old province of Asia, the Byzantine rite must be attached to Syria; and the political prestige of Constantinople little by little carried this composite rite all over the Byzantine empire and well beyond its frontiers, notably to the Slavs whose states grew up within the cultural and political orbit of the New Rome.

It was the two great Syrian centres, Antioch and Jerusalem, that had the decisive part in the final formation of the Byzantine rite. The see of Constantinople was several times occupied by bishops of Antiochene origin during the fourth–sixth centuries: and this was a decisive period for the formation of liturgies, for it was a time of intensive doctrinal and disciplinary activity and of many important councils, the time, too, that saw the growth of the patriarchal system which characterizes the Christian East. It was also a time when pilgrims were flocking to the Holy Places, not only Jerusalem and those of Palestine, but also the basilicas of SS. Sergius and Bacchus at Resapha, in the heart of Syria, and of St Simeon Stylites, "the pillar-man", in the extreme north, not far from

Antioch. To meet the religious needs of pilgrims and to commemorate the historical events of man's redemption at the very places where they happened, Jerusalem was the first Church to evolve a cycle of feasts; this doubtless began when St Cyril was bishop there (348–86), and it influenced the whole Christian world.

But the most important and lasting liturgical work was that done in the Palestinian monasteries, especially in the *laura* of Mar Saba, founded in 478 in a wild gorge of the Cedron, about nine miles from Jerusalem, by St Sabas, the favourite disciple of St Euthymius. It was at Mar Saba, during the eighth century, that a group of monks from Syria originated the *kanon* form of hymnody, which gradually superseded the older *kontakion* form, also of Syrian origin. The master of the *kontakion*[12] was St Romanus the Singer, who was born at Emesa (Homs) at the beginning of the sixth century and was a deacon first at Beirut and then at Constantinople. He made use of the poetical forms and themes popularized over a century before in East Syria by St Ephrem and his followers. St Andrew of Crete, born at Damascus and a monk of Mar Saba, as were his compatriots and imitators St John Damascene and St Cosmas of Maiuma a little later, no doubt got his idea of the *kanon* from the series of antiphons in use at Antioch: strophes (*troparia*) to be inserted between the verses of the biblical canticles at the morning office. This literary form was soon introduced at Constantinople, with the Mar Saba service-books, and there it had an astonishing success, especially at the monastery of Studius, which was linked with Mar Saba in upholding sacred images against Iconoclasm. It is to Studite monks, the abbot St Theodore, St Joseph the Hymnwriter and Theophanes, that is attributed the definitive editing of the books now used for the Divine Office of the Byzantine rite: the *Typikon*, or general rules, the *Oktoekhos* and *Parakletike* for the Sunday and weekday office, the *Trio-*

---

[12] *Kontakion*: a succession of lines of equal length grouped in regular acrostic stanzas.

dion for Lent and the *Pentekostarion* for paschaltime. After the defeat of Iconoclasm this monastic office supplanted the old cathedral office, of which, however, many traces can be found among the Armenians.

Documents antedating this disturbed period have almost all disappeared, and the history of the Byzantine rite can be followed only from about the second half of the eighth century. In the spring of 842 sacred images were finally restored, and this was marked by the institution of the feast of Orthodoxy (first Sunday in Lent) to celebrate the overcoming of all previous heresies; this date was the beginning of a time of liturgical unification and regulation throughout the empire. From now on the eucharistic liturgy called "of St John Chrysostom", whose Antiochene origin is undeniable, tended to displace the ancient anaphora "of St Basil": this was perhaps of Egyptian origin, but Basil certainly seems to have given it its final form. The liturgy of the sacraments (contained in the book called *Eukhologion*) owes a lot to Antiochene tradition, except for the wedding service, in which local customs were dominant.

In the centuries that followed, especially between the twelfth and the fifteenth, excessive attention was given to secondary observances, such as the preparation of the bread and wine (*prothesis*) before the eucharistic liturgy. The deacon's part was regulated down to the last detail, for it had become very important: the deacon had to lead the people's prayer, for they could no longer see the celebrant. This was because a closed screen, covered with icons, now hid the altar; this iconostasis was another borrowing from Syria. The celebrant got into the habit of saying the greater part of the priestly prayer in a low voice, whilst the people sang hymns and responded to the invocations of the deacon's litanies. Thus at this late date the Byzantine rite acquired the form in which it is still celebrated. Its evolution was not unlike that which was going on during the same period in the West, where choir-screens were being put up and the people were getting more and more out of touch with the liturgy, which had become an exclusively clerical affair. But there was no break like that in the East, because the congregation still understood the language used at public worship and the deacon's litanies were an integral part of the celebration; the people's hymns, too, were simply a development of older "acclamations": whereas in the West the devotional practices that grew up were simply juxtaposed to the liturgical rite.

From the twelfth century the use of this truly ecumenical[13] liturgy spread to all parts of the Byzantine empire, including the other orthodox patriarchates. Its adoption by Antioch is easily understood, for it was largely of Antiochene origin. The orthodox patriarchate of Alexandria, on the other hand, was for a long time no more than a legal fiction; yet even so it did not give up its traditional liturgy without a struggle and without the considered opinion of a patriarch of Antioch who was an outstanding canonist, Theodore Balsamon.

For a long time, too, there had been an unforeseen expansion of the Byzantine rite outside the empire. This was largely due to the enterprise of two missionaries who came out of Constantinople at the time of the patriarch Photius and of Popes Nicholas I and Adrian II: St Cyril (christened Constantine) and his brother St Methodius. It was within the ambit of the Roman liturgical tradition, in Moravia, that they first began to use Slavonic for liturgical and biblical purposes, a language that up till then (863–66) had not been written down. But when they and their followers were called to evangelize heathen people within Constantinople's sphere of interest they returned to the Byzantine rite, and the activities of Western clergy for long spoiled their bold move in the Roman rite, although it had been solemnly approved by Pope John VIII in 879 and by the patriarch Photius in 881.

A century later, in 988, the baptism of the prince of Kiev, St Vladimir, opened a new province to the Byzantine rite,

[13] In the sense, given to this word in the Byzantine world, of conterminous with the empire.

one that was to become a huge empire. Up till then there had been only occasional missions into Russia, but now the Church began to be solidly organized there, forming a new Christian people with the aid of her liturgy above all. It would be difficult to exaggerate the part played by the monasteries in this: first the *laura* of the Caves at Kiev, founded about 1052 by St Antony Pechersky and his disciple St Theodosius, and then the countless centres of monastic life, hermitages and communities, that sprang up all over the land to the Arctic Ocean. The liturgy was celebrated in the people's tongue, and with singing inspired by the old native music. Apart from a few special usages, public worship long retained its original form, without the innovations introduced at Constantinople; but this led to an upheaval when, having become a patri-archate, Moscow began to look upon itself as the centre of Orthodoxy and heir to the authentic Byzantine tradition. Re-garding the maintenance of the old usages as infidelity, the patriarch Nikon resolved at a synod held in Moscow in 1654 to carry out a general correction of the Russian liturgical books to bring them into line with those of the Greeks. The people were deeply shocked by this, for they identified their traditional customs with the purity of the Orthodox faith. A schism (*raskol*) took place, which was to weigh heavily on Russia's religious future; but in the meantime a synod in 1666 formally adopted Nikon's reform.

By the Union of Brest in 1595 the western dioceses of the province of Kiev (then in Polish hands) had confirmed the reunion with Rome entered into by the metropolitan Isidore at the Council of Florence. This meant that these parts were not affected by Nikon's liturgical reforms, but on the other hand certain Western usages were adopted in the course of time. The result was a rather hybrid liturgy (sometimes called "uniat") which is still in use among the Catholic Ruthenians (Ukrainians and others), whom the events of the past fifty years have scattered over western Europe and, especially, North America. There has been much less "latinizing" among the Catholic Melkites, who have retained interesting vestiges of some archaic usages. These modifications, like those among the Catholic Rumanians and Bulgars, do not alter the deep unity of the Byzantine rite as it is revealed in all its splendour at a concelebration, when the different celebrants sometimes officiate each in his own language, and the diversity of chant further witnesses to the diversity of civilizations that are here united in one and the same faith.

The Armenian liturgy

It has already been explained how Armenia came to have a special liturgy, a most distinctive synthesis of Syrian and Cappadocian elements within a framework borrowed from Jerusalem. Attention may be drawn to the existing resemblances between the Armenian rite and the old liturgy of Constantinople before it was remodelled under the influence of Palestinian monasteries: but there is no doubt that this older Byzantine liturgy already owed much to the great sanctuaries of Jerusalem.

Syrian influence, more precisely, the East Syrian influence of Edessa, is particularly marked in the Armenian calendar. Today it is the only one which has practically no feasts with fixed dates: there are but six of them, and of these, three have been introduced since the thirteenth century and under Western influence. Other feasts are allotted to certain days of the week: Sunday is reserved for feasts of our Lord only, as are Friday, sacred to the Passion, and Wednesday, sacred to the Incarnation. Apart from Armenian saints, the calendar of saints is confined almost entirely to Palestinian, Syrian and Persian names.

There is only one form of the eucharistic liturgy in the Armenian rite, and it goes under the name of St Athanasius of Alexandria. It is in fact an adaptation of the old anaphora called "of St Basil", which may well have originated in Egypt before it was theologically developed by St Basil in Cappadocia. Other anaphoras, Byzantine, Armenian or Syro-

Armenian, have long gone out of use. Among all the Eastern Churches, that of Armenia is peculiar in that, from early times, it uses unleavened bread in the Eucharist, instead of the usual leavened. In the theological controversies between Orthodox and Armenians attempts have been made to give this custom a doctrinal significance which it has not got; but it is likely that the persistent antagonism between Constantinople and Armenia helped to confirm the Armenians in their own observance. Also, alone among all ancient Churches, that of Armenia does not add water to the eucharistic wine, in face of a tradition universal since the second century. The Armenians claim that this was originally done in opposition to Judaeo-Christian sects, such as the Ebionites, which consecrated pure water on account of their false beliefs about wine.

Apart from these peculiarities, the Armenian liturgy was also considerably influenced over the centuries, first, by developments in the Byzantine rite, and then from the West at the Crusades. In spite of its attribution to the catholicos Mashdots in the ninth century, the Ritual is not in fact older than the twelfth. Thus it came about that certain Franco-Roman usages were introduced during the existence of the Armenian kingdom of Cilicia, and through the activities of Dominican friars and the affiliated Armenian Brothers of Unity; these affected the dissidents as well as the Catholics, but in later times the Catholics have become yet more latinized. The astonishing plasticity of the Armenian character and the migrations which have established their communities in western Europe and America have also helped to attenuate the distinctiveness of a liturgy that had such very various origins.

THE ALEXANDRIAN LITURGICAL FAMILY

The Coptic rite

Egypt has always been noted for "going its own way", and for its ability to assimilate and transform to its own pattern all sorts of "foreignnesses". In its origin and in its history Alexandria is apart from the rest of the country, an artificial city open to the sea on one side, cut off by lagoons and desert on the others. This situation had a bad effect on Christian Egypt, in spite of the intellectual prestige of the Hellenistic city and the great ability of its patriarchs: from the time of St Athanasius these men could count on the support of a numerous body of monks all over the country, and they sometimes had the look of "ecclesiastical Pharaohs", anxious and able to stand up to the religious and social policies of imperial Constantinople. After the Council of Chalcedon, this nationalist opposition claimed the theological patronage of the great Alexandrian bishop St Cyril, who had been the outstanding figure at the Council of Ephesus.

The old eucharistic liturgy of the see of St Mark, translated into Coptic, continued in use under Cyril's name. But the influence of the monks became more and more exclusive. It was not only the Divine Office which, more than anywhere else, was celebrated according to monastic ideas, with prolonged psalmody, a pronounced biblical character, and a repugnance for external observances: the development of the *whole* liturgy received the stamp. But there was also Syrian influence, greater than is often recognized. The Jacobite Church kept its vitality until the fifteenth century, in a way the Coptic Church did not. All the doctrinal and liturgical development took place in Syria, and it was Syrian monks (especially those of St Mary's in the desert of Skete) who transmitted it to Egypt; for several centuries the country lived, religiously speaking, largely on Syrian imports.

But during the twelfth and thirteenth centuries a succession of vigorous patriarchs carried through a big reform. The Bohairic dialect of the Delta became more and more exclusively used, and this entailed the forgetting and disappearance of foreign formularies, which had mostly been translated into the Sahidic dialect of Upper Egypt. The reforming provisions of canon law and the great encyclopedia of Abd-ul-Barakat (fourteenth century) fixed the details of the revision of the liturgical books at this time, and the present form of the Ritual is due to the patriarch Gabriel V in the following century. There are now three eucharistic anaphoras, and in practice that "of St Basil" is preferred to the old Alexandrian anaphora "of St Cyril", which is too long and very difficult to sing. To a large extent, Syrian forms are in use for the sacraments, but the Divine Office and the calendar keep their traditional shapes: at most, along with the ancient *troparia* and certain local compositions, Syrian office hymns are in use, particularly *Theotokia*; these hymns to our Lady for the time before Christmas are still very popular.

For a long time Arabic has been more and more used in liturgical services, side by side with Coptic, and some chants and acclamations are always in Greek: but it may be said that, beneath these various disguises, the Coptic liturgy still remains as it was fixed by the monks of Dair Makarios in the Wadi Natrun in the days when the patriarchs of Alexandria lived among them.

The Ethiopian liturgy

The liturgy of Ethiopia is a daughter of that of the Copts, but keeping more Syrian elements. Did not the country's first evangelizers come from Roman Syria? And no doubt the maintenance of this element was encouraged by returning pilgrims and by the monks at Jerusalem at the time of the great Ethiopic revival in the fourteenth and fifteenth centuries. That Jewish traditions and legends had a place in this revival is well known, and it is possible that they went back to the far-off days of the first Axumite kings. However that may be, it is certain that the Ethiopian liturgy is a very distinctive one.

Among the seventeen anaphoras included in the recent edition of the Missal there are transcriptions, or rather adaptations, of Coptic ones, while others have come, directly or not, from Syria. What is surprising is to find the old Roman anaphora of Hippolytus still in use, transmitted through the so-called apostolic canons, which had more influence in Ethiopia than anywhere else. There are also native Ethiopian compositions, especially in the hymnary, and a remarkable adaptation to local taste and customs of rites borrowed from places widely separated in the Christian world. The Ethiopian liturgy is almost unexplored, yet it is of unusual importance both from an historical and a pastoral point of view.

CHAPTER IV

THE GENIUS OF THE EASTERN RITES

In a masterly study Edmund Bishop expounded the genius of the Roman rite and its distinctive characteristics.[1] For the Western Christian, the genius of the Eastern rites is marked in the first place by opposite characteristics. The Roman liturgy is outstandingly sober and simple: the more symbolical, complex and striking of its observances have been brought into it from outside, notably from Frankish lands; such are the original Palm Sunday and Easter fire observances, the rites of ordination and for the dedication of a church. Others originated in Syria or Jerusalem, whence they were carried into Gaul and Spain; yet others were first used in the papal liturgy, at the time when this drew its inspiration from the gorgeous ceremonial of the sacred imperial palace at Constantinople.

It has already been remarked that the Western observer of any Eastern liturgy is at once struck by two things: the length and complexity of the service, and the atmosphere of sacredness in which it takes place, yet a sacredness that is accompanied by a sense of ease and familiarity. The deacon keeps attention on the alert, he prompts the assembly ("Stand up!" "Draw near ... !"), he invites to prayer and indicates responses. Whereas at first sight the Roman liturgy appears to be "aristocratic". Not that it deliberately excludes a single

[1] Printed in *Liturgia historica* (Oxford, 1918).

member of the gathering—on the contrary, it is highly congregational, and no other rite makes so much of the priestly function of the whole Christian people: but it does it with such moderation, with such dignity and decorum, that for long centuries the liturgy was esteemed to be a function solely of the clergy.

The East has been spared any such misfortune. We have seen that its existing liturgies mostly grew out of celebrations in small towns and villages, and under the influence of monks who never lost close contact with the common people from whom they were for the most part drawn. The majority of these monks were illiterate, men not in holy orders and little inclined to bother about rubrical refinements. Only the Byzantine liturgy escaped this state of affairs, as it also escaped (until after it had been given its definitive form) the humiliating situation of Churches that had been reduced to minority status in an Islamic state, where the official religion knew public prayer only as a very bare and simple thing. And it came about that Constantinople, to its already grandiose heritage from Antioch and Jerusalem, added a ceremonial which transposed worship of the *Pantokrator*, the All-Mighty, into the pomp of the court of the *Basileus*, the Emperor. But the liturgy's communal or popular basis remained, and developed in the Slav lands, and even in Turkish-dominated Greece. It was associated with a very powerful sense of mystery, which was first manifested in Antiochene Syria, giving a Christian twist to that tremulous adoration of the Incomprehensible to which the East is called: a vocation which, notwithstanding diversity of temperaments, civilizations and historical destinies, differentiates the East from a West that becomes less and less sensitive to mystery.

But these common traits are modified according to the cultures and to the liturgies to which they gave birth. There are liturgies of speech and liturgies of action, those which in various ways give expression to feeling and those which in the first place encourage inward contemplation, liturgies which stress divine transcendence and mystery and others which emphasize the merciful purposes of God, "the lover of man".

The East Syrian liturgy is the simplest and most archaic known to traditional Christianity. It was evolved, and soon reached its fixed form, in surroundings wherein Jewish influences were strong, where from the earliest times Christian communities had a semi-monastic organization, and in an area beyond the Roman world and its exuberant civilization. The territories of the catholicate of Seleucia were never Christian: in Persia, in central Asia and India, the relatively small Christian communities were all but lost in an ocean of infidels. Whatever the factors that conditioned this liturgy, its austerity is striking: the celebration begins with the Lord's Prayer, there are biblical readings and rhythmical homilies, rather like commentaries or glosses, with no rhetorical graces, and these alternate with lengthy monotonous psalmody, the whole taking place in front of a plain wall, with one door, cutting off sight of the altar. As in synagogues, the old churches were dominated by the *bema*, a large platform in the middle of the building; this was the clergy's place, and the lessons were read from it. Sacramental rites are reduced to a minimum and there is little external ceremony, not even in Holy Week, when the rest of Christendom is using those evocative observances that originated in Jerusalem. It is a liturgy of meditation, of listening to the word, of quietness and simplicity—no wonder that it struck an answering note in the souls of the people of India.

The Coptic liturgy is not dissimilar, but for different reasons. It is a monastic liturgy, slow and excessively long, with strange, solemn chants that the singers vary as they will and hymns whose rhythms are marked by clashing cymbals. Again there is little external ceremony, but some expressive gestures, such as the outstretched hands at the Lord's Prayer and the bare feet of the celebrant at the altar. The sanctuary is called the holy place (*haikal*) that it is, cut off from the nave by a lattice screen that carries a few icons. Perhaps more

than at any other liturgy, the congregation actively joins in
it throughout.

The Coptic liturgy has been considerably influenced by that
of Antioch, where, with Jerusalem—two cities that are in-
separable in liturgical history—public worship took on the
finest symbolism: all was directed to the showing forth of an
unutterable mystery, to making a presence felt. More than any
other, the Syrian liturgy is directed towards the last things,
intent on that Parousia, that Second Coming, which is already
with us through the sacraments. It has been pointed out how
important a part hymns soon had at Antioch: they deck every
celebration in a poetic mantle which helps the participants
to enter into its mystery. From Jerusalem came those observances, whose symbolism everyone can understand, which
make the decisive moments of our redemption alive and
present to us. This liturgy is intensely human; in this respect
very close to that of the West in the Middle Ages with its
spontaneity and drama, but more successful in keeping the
sacred character of the mystery. Its genius for expressive
symbolism reaches its highest point in Holy Week, but among
the Maronites that has unhappily been spoilt by a feeble
naturalism, due probably to foreign influence.

Antioch, too, contributed several of its distinctive characteristics to the Byzantine rite, and they were refined and
extended to produce a truly imperial and world-wide liturgy,
in which Greek moderation and balance have tempered the
exuberance of Syrian and Asian Hellenism. Different as it is
from that of Old Rome, the liturgy of New Rome is also a
wonderful flower of Mediterranean civilization transfigured
by Christianity, a work fashioned by the genius of prechristian
and Christian Hellenism. But it was destined to find a new
vitality in Slav lands. Not that it underwent important changes
there: on the contrary, we have seen that the Slavonic version
was very traditionalist, and that when there was a systematic
revision in Russia it was to bring it into line with contemporary Greek usage.

But the deeply contemplative piety of the Slavs, their gifts for pictorial and musical expression, gave the Byzantine liturgy a new guise in which it is known today all over the world. The schools of Novgorod and Moscow developed the art of the icon, and these pictures became a part of the celebration whose master ideas they sum up. The traditional sacred images had for long been regarded as holy in a special way, but up till then neither Constantinople nor Greece had projected into them the rites and texts in which the Church relives the mystery of Easter transfiguration. The musical chant which soon evolved at Kiev was the basis of those fine compositions of the eighteenth–nineteenth century masters which still form the ordinary repertoire of Russian and Ukrainian choirs.

It is by its appointments and singing that the Armenian liturgy, too, marks its particular quality in the first place. The absence of a picture-screen, and often even of curtains about the altar, means that one gets the full effect of the movements of the numerous ministers in their stately vestments. The liturgy is solemn and recollected, and a little mournful, qualities that are enhanced by the specially beautiful chant. The Armenian rite may appear rather closer than others to us of the Roman rite, because of its borrowings from the West: but it is also faithful to the solid sobriety of the ancient liturgy of Caesarea or Antioch before the magnificent but rather overpowering developments of the Byzantine Middle Ages.

CHAPTER V

THE RITES OF CHRISTIAN INITIATION: BAPTISM AND CONFIRMATION

In the Eastern Churches the liturgy of Christian initiation follows the earliest tradition of the universal Church, whereas the rituals that we Westerners know have all been drawn up for babies and not for adults. Baptism is given by total or partial immersion, accompanied among the Syrians, Chaldeans and Armenians by a pouring of water on the head; it is at once followed by an anointing with oil on the forehead, and sometimes on other parts of the body, as the sacrament of "the seal of the Holy Spirit" (confirmation). The custom of immediately giving communion to the newly-baptized has also been maintained, except by the Chaldeans, who have no trace of it, and the Maronites, who allow it only for adult neophytes.

The baptismal ritual is generally modelled on that of the eucharistic liturgy, as is particularly noticeable among the Chaldeans and Copts. The place of the consecratory anaphora is taken by the blessing of the baptismal water, accompanied (except among the Syrians and Maronites) by the blessing of the oil, but the biblical readings occur all over the place: at the beginning of the rite (Syrians and Maronites), during the immediate preparation for baptism (Chaldeans, Copts, Armenians), or just before the communion (Byzantines). In the texts of the Syrian, Coptic, Armenian and Byzantine rites, an ancient source can be detected, doubtless Antiochene; and another, quite different, in the Chaldean. The baptismal formula itself is generally enunciative: "N. *is baptized* in the name . . .", with variations that will be noted later.

The oldest forms of baptismal ritual known to us are in Syria, through the *Didascalia Apostolorum* and its adaptation to more developed conditions in the *Apostolic Constitutions*, and through the catechetical lessons of Cyril of Jerusalem, Theodore of Mopsuestia and John Chrysostom (cf. p. 36). Theodore's catecheses are in the form of a commentary on a ritual whose text is quoted and then explained sentence by sentence. The end of Book vii of the *Apostolic Constitutions* has preserved a valuable collection of prayers and admonitions that have a strong flavour of antiquity. All these documents stress the importance of the anointing with oil which precedes baptism, and careful directions are given on how it is to be done. The whole body is anointed "in sign of spiritual baptism", says the *Apostolic Constitutions*. The declaration of renouncement of Satan and adherence to Christ, about which Theodore of Mopsuestia is particularly explicit, is also detailed at length. But the anointing *after* baptism does not figure in several documents, and only Cyril of Jerusalem gives it full weight: it is to be done with perfumed oil (*myron*) on the forehead, ears, nostrils and chest, and is referred to the coming of the Holy Spirit upon Christ after his baptism in the Jordan. The ritual in the *Apostolic Constitutions* simply prays that "the sweet fragrance of Christ may continue strong and unabated in the baptized person, and that after dying with Christ he may rise and live with him". Theodore speaks only of signing the forehead in the name of the Father, of the Son and of the Holy Spirit.

At the present day the baptismal rituals are of two types. One is proper to the East Syrians, and is said to have been put into order by the catholicos Ishu'yab III, who reorganized the Nestorian liturgy in the seventh century. The other is used by the Jacobite Church (which knows more than one version), by the Coptic Church and by the Byzantines. The Jacobite versions go under the names of the patriarch Severus († 538) and of James of Edessa († 708); there is reason to think that James translated an older Antiochene ritual into Syriac, probably adapting it. Did this carry the mark of Severus? It is possible; but in its present form it represents a later stage of the liturgy, when baptism of adults was no longer in use. The Coptic rite of today bears more traces of a time when the catechumenate was still a living reality.

FIRST PREPARATORY RITES

The child is made a catechumen by being signed with the cross,[1] sometimes joined with an anointing with oil or a laying on of hands. No Eastern rite has the African and Roman custom of giving the child salt. Under the title "Prayer at giving a name on the eighth day after birth", the Byzantine ritual has kept a formula that is known to the Syrians and Maronites and was at one time used by the Armenians:

> O Lord our God, we pray and beseech you that the light of your countenance may rest on this your servant, and that your Son's cross may be impressed on his heart and his mind, that he may flee the vanity of the world and the snares of the Enemy and may keep your commandments. Let your holy name, Lord, rest on hîm without denial, for he is in due time to be joined to your holy Church and admitted to the awe-full mysteries of your Christ: so that after living in accordance with your commandments and having kept your seal inviolate, he may receive the happiness of the chosen ones in your kingdom. . . .

In the present Byzantine ritual the catechumen, head and feet bare, clad in a shirt, facing the east, is thrice breathed on and thrice signed with the cross. Then come a prayer with laying on of hands and a threefold exorcism. The Armenians have only the imposition of hands and its prayer, but the Catholic ritual has revived the old usage of saying Psalm 131,

[1] Originally this signing seems to have recalled the sign T (*tau*), which is the mark of the elect according to Ezechiel (9. 4) and the Apocalypse (7. 3).

"Lord, remember David". Syrians and Maronites have only the breathing and the triple signing on the brow, to which the Copts add an anointing. But these last three rites introduce the catechumenate with chants, prayers and (except the Copts) readings on the pattern of the beginning of the eucharistic liturgy. The Chaldean rite retains no trace of the catechumenate, but it is known from ancient documents that it used to include imposition of hands and signing with the cross. The following is the Byzantine "Prayer for making a catechumen":

> In your name, Lord God of truth, and of your only-begotten Son and of your Holy Spirit, I lay my hand on your servant N., who has been accounted worthy to turn to your name and to be shielded under your wings. Take away the primeval fault from him and fill him with faith, hope and charity towards you. May he understand that you alone are God, you and your only-begotten Son Jesus Christ, our Lord, and your Holy Spirit. Let him walk in the way of your commandments and do what is pleasing to you, for the man who does these things shall live. Enter him in your book of life, join him to the flock that is yours; may your holy name and of your well-beloved Son Jesus Christ, our Lord, and of your holy life-giving Spirit be glorified in him. May your eyes ever look on him mercifully, and your ears be open to his prayer. Gladden him by the work of your hands and in all his kindred, that he may confess you by magnifying and glorifying your high and holy name, ceaselessly praising you all the days of his life. For it is you whom the heavenly powers acclaim, yours is the glory, Father, Son and Holy Spirit, now and always and for ever and ever. Amen.

RENOUNCEMENT OF SATAN; PROFESSION OF FAITH

A renouncement of Satan is attested by the earliest documents, which indicate that it should be made facing west. Some follow it at once by a promise to cleave henceforth to Christ, and this is done towards the east because there the dawn breaks, and Christ is the true light of the world. But as early as the *Apostolic Tradition* of Hippolytus this decisive action is preceded by a vigil service of readings and instructions, begun by a last exorcism with breathing on and signing of the chief parts of the body. These rites are still found in the Byzantine liturgy, with a prayer as follows[2]:

> Lord and Master, you created man in your own image and likeness and gave him power to attain everlasting life; and afterwards you did not reject him when he fell by sinning, but instead you brought about the world's salvation through the incarnation of your Son. You have delivered this creature of yours here from slavery to the Enemy: receive him now into your heavenly kingdom. Open the eyes of his understanding that the light of your Gospel may shine in him; give him an angel of light to go with him and deliver him from every wile of the Adversary, from encountering the Evil One, the noonday demon and any illusions of iniquity. Drive away every evil and impure spirit that lurks in his heart (*thrice*): the spirit of error, the spirit of self-will, the spirit of idolatry and of endless covetousness, the spirit of falsehood and of every wickedness that the Devil instigates. Make him an understanding (*logike*) sheep in the holy flock of your Christ, an honourable member of your Church, a holy vessel, a child of light and an inheritor of your kingdom: so that after living in accordance with your commandments and having kept your seal inviolate and his robe unspotted, he may receive the happiness of your holy ones in your kingdom. . . .

There is no such explicit form of exorcism among the Armenians, and it has disappeared from the Chaldean rite; but these two rites have kept some of the psalmody of the former vigil. The Armenians say Psalms 24, 25 and 50 before the renouncement; the Chaldeans, who have lost both the renouncement[3] and the profession of faith, begin the baptismal

---

[2] An amplified form of this prayer is found in the Coptic rite, but it comes after the profession of faith.

[3] The Catholic Chaldeans have restored it, immediately before the prebaptismal anointing.

office with Psalm 83, followed by laying on of hands and a prayer. The Syrians and Maronites bring together here a series of exorcisms which were formerly distributed throughout the catechumate, like those which remain in the Roman and Byzantine rites.

The form of the renunciation of Satan has been maintained very consistently from the earliest documents.[4] In the Byzantine and Armenian rites it takes the form of question and answer, and the first requires the catechumen (or the godparent) to express his horror of Satan by blowing and spitting towards the west, as if to expel all trace of corruption. The Syrian, Maronite and Coptic rites make use of a formula of which the Syrian version is the most restrained; it runs: "I, N., renounce Satan, and all his service and all his works, all his pomps, all his worldly falsehood, and all those who serve and follow him."

The Byzantines, Syrians and Copts make an explicit declaration of future faithfulness to Christ; the Armenians express faith in the Triune God. Like the renunciation of Satan, adherence to Christ can be expressed by way of interrogation (Byzantines) or of declaration (Syrians, Copts); the Byzantine dialogue is:

Q. Do you join yourself to Christ?
A. I join myself to him.
Q. Are you joined to Christ?
A. I am joined to him.
Q. Do you believe in him?
A. I believe in him as King and God. I believe in one God, the Father almighty, etc. (the Nicene Creed, which is repeated twice more).
Q. Are you joined to Christ?
A. I am joined to him.
Q. Worship him then.
A. I worship the Father, the Son and the Holy Spirit, the consubstantial and indivisible Trinity.

[4] The variations can be explained by accidental doublings or faulty translation of a primitive formula in Aramaic.

Except the Chaldean, all rites have a profession of faith here, which among the Copts has kept its primitive shortness: "I believe in one God, the Father almighty, and in his only Son, Jesus Christ our Lord, and in the life-giving Holy Spirit, in the resurrection of the body, and in the one holy, catholic and apostolic Church." Other rites use the Symbol of Nicaea.

CONSECRATION OF THE WATER; ANOINTING; BAPTISM

After this preparatory "catechumenate" comes the liturgy of baptism proper. It is specially impressive, because in the Eastern rites the consecration of the water always, and the blessing of the oil of catechumens sometimes, takes place at this point. In the Maronite, Chaldean and Coptic rites this baptismal liturgy is modelled on the eucharistic liturgy, the consecration of the water[5] taking the place of the anaphora. While going to the baptistery the Armenians sing the Easter Psalm 117, and they have the biblical readings between the blessing of the oil and the consecration of the water. The Byzantine rite has transferred the readings to before the communion, but it has a litany here and the priest, fully vested, says a prayer: candles are alight and the thurible smoking. The Syrians are content with two candles, one on either side of the baptismal vessel, on which a cross is laid, and the priest's prayer is shorter than the Byzantine one: "Lord God, you who entrusted to your apostles this spiritual ministry of baptizing in water and the Spirit, perfect this person now ready for holy baptism, through the agency of me, your sinful servant. Shining with the gifts of the Holy Spirit received from you, may he be sealed by that Spirit and inscribed among the children of your grace; and may he give you the glory that is your due, with your Father and your Holy Spirit, now and always and for ever and ever."

[5] In the Chaldean rite the consecration of the oil of anointing, which in the older tradition took the place of chrism.

The Syrian, Maronite and Chaldean rites here have a first anointing on the forehead; this usage is already described in Theodore of Mopsuestia's ritual, and it may have originated in a doubling of the primitive rite: the bishop anointed the brow and the deacon extended it to the whole body. In the Syrian rite the words are: "N. is signed with the oil of gladness, that he may be armed against the Enemy and grafted into the whole olive-tree, in God's holy, catholic and apostolic Church." The Coptic rite, in which the catechumen is undressed when he arrives at the baptistery, puts the prebaptismal anointing before the consecration of the water; as there is an anointing at the very beginning of the office, the oil has already been blessed there. Armenians and Chaldeans put this blessing before that of the water, and Byzantines immediately before oil is poured into the water.

Whether or not the blessing of the oil is joined with it, the consecration of the water is a most impressive rite. Among the Syrians the prayer of consecration is preceded by two others and by a chant referring to the baptism of Christ: "John prepared the baptismal waters, and Christ made them holy. He went down into them and was baptized. When he came out of them, the heavens and the earth bowed before him. The sun lowered its rays and the stars worshipped him who had sanctified all springs and rivers."

A form of consecration, perhaps dating from the fourth century, has come down with varying modifications to the Byzantine, Armenian, Syrian, Maronite and Coptic rites of today, one used not only at baptism but at the blessing of the waters on the Epiphany. It has been kept in a particularly pure state by the Syrians and, the last part of it, in an old Byzantine formula. Here it is, as reconstructed from these sources:

Lord, God almighty, creator of all things, seen and unseen, you made heaven and earth and all that is in them; you drew the waters together into one, and the earth appeared; you shut the abyss and keep it shut; you separated the waters that are above the heavens.

Your power kept the sea in its place, and crushed the heads of the monsters of the deep [Psalm 73. 13]. You are mighty—who can stand before you? Lord, look now on your creature, this water. Give it a saving grace, the blessing of Jordan, the consecration of the Holy Spirit. Drive out of it everything that is harmful, for your great and glorious name, fearsome to the Enemy, has been invoked on it. We glorify you and your only-begotten Son and your Holy Spirit, now and always and for ever and ever. Amen.

May all hostile powers be broken by the sign, symbol of the cross of your Christ. May the invisible phantoms of the air be driven off, no dark spirit lurk in these waters. We pray, Lord, that when he who is to be baptized goes into them, the unclean spirit of darkness may not go with him, darkening the mind and confusing the intellect. Rather, Lord of all, make this water here a water of rest, a water of redemption, a water of sanctification; a cleansing of body and spirit, a freeing from bondage, a forgiveness of sins, an enlightening of the soul; a bath of rebirth, gift of adoption, garment of incorruptibility, renewal of mind, source of life. You, Lord, said, "Wash, and be made clean"; take away evil from your people, you who have given us new birth from on high through water and the Spirit. Be upon this water, Lord, and transfigure those who are washed in it, that they may put off the old self, rotten with corrupt passions, and put on the new self, reborn in the image of him who created them. In baptism made like your only-begotten Son, may they have part in his resurrection. Having kept the gift of the Holy Spirit and increased in grace, may they be rewarded with the summons to Heaven and there be counted among its first-born, in you, our God and Lord, Jesus Christ.

In the Coptic rite this prayer follows the pattern of a eucharistic anaphora. After Scripture readings there are "universal" prayers and a threefold form of supplication; after the usual dialogue, a preface hymns God's power and glory, ending with "Holy, holy, holy . . ."; the middle part, in the form of two long prayers, is followed by the Lord's Prayer and the pouring of chrism into the water while psalms are sung. Then comes the baptism itself, in the place of the communion. In the Chaldean rite the consecration of the oil is the middle part of the anaphora, the blessing of the water, by a very simple formula, coming after the Lord's Prayer. All rites prescribe the pouring of a little chrism or oil into the baptismal water, except the Chaldean, which simply directs that the sign of the cross be made over the water with the phial of oil, with the words: "This water is signed and sanctified with holy oil . . .". When the baptismal ritual is modelled on the eucharistic service, this consecration or pouring corresponds to the consecration of the bread and wine.

The anointing of the catechumen just before baptism is very old, and general since the third century. It is therefore surprising that it does not occur in the Armenian rite, which nevertheless has a blessing of the oil which explicitly refers to it: it is a very ancient formula, closely related to that in the *Apostolic Tradition* of Hippolytus which has left traces in the Roman and Coptic rites: "O God, with a good and holy oil you anointed priests, prophets and kings. Now, compassionate Lord, we ask you to send the grace of your Holy Spirit on this oil, that to him who is anointed with it may be given the blessing of spiritual wisdom bravely to fight and overcome the Adversary." For the whole tradition of this prebaptismal anointing is that it is in preparation for warfare: it strengthens the catechumen for his supreme conflict with the powers of evil; probably the Syrians are only maintaining ancient usage when they do not distinguish between oil of catechumens and oil of the sick, for in either case the powers of evil are involved.

And now at last comes the baptism itself. As has been said, it is generally given by total or partial immersion. Among the Byzantines it is total, three times, with the words: "The servant of God N. is baptized in the name of the Father and of the Son and of the Holy Spirit." In the Armenian rite the child is first held in the font while the priest pours water with his hand over its head, saying: "The servant of God N., of his own will coming to baptism from the state of being a catechumen, is now baptized in the name of the Father and of the Son and of the Holy Spirit." Then he immerses the child completely, three times, saying: "Being ransomed from the slavery of sin by Christ's blood and set free by the heavenly Father's power, he becomes a co-heir with Christ and a temple of the Holy Spirit."

Among the Syrians and Maronites the water is poured three times with the left hand while the right rests on the child's head. The Syrian formula is: "N. is baptized in the name of the Father and of the Son and of the Holy Spirit unto everlasting life"; but the Maronite formula, following the Roman use, is active: "N., I baptize you, lamb of Christ's flock, in the name of the Father and of the Son and of the Holy Spirit unto everlasting life." In the Chaldean rite the child is put in the water up to its neck and the head immersed three times, with the words: "N. is baptized in the name of the Father and of the Son and of the Holy Spirit, for eternity." The Copts have three immersions, after each of which the priest breathes on the child's face: their formula has been active from early times, but it is divided into three phrases to correspond with the immersions: "N., I baptize you in the name of the Father; in the name of the Son; and in the name of the Holy Spirit. Amen."

The Byzantine neophyte is at once clothed in the "garment of righteousness", while Psalm 31 is sung, "Blessed are they who have their faults forgiven, their trangressions buried deep", followed by the chant (*troparion*): "Grant me a robe of light, you who are clothed in light as with a garment, all-merciful Christ, our God." In the Chaldean rite the neophyte simply receives back his ordinary clothes, but in other rites he is not dressed again till after confirmation. The Syrians sing the following lines of St Ephrem whilst the newly-baptized is being dried: "Stretch forth your wings, holy Church, and welcome the gentle lambs begotten by the Holy Spirit in the waters of baptism. Come in peace, you lambs new-born in baptism, brought from the water's womb in the name of the Trinity." (The Coptic and Chaldean rites have a prayer here for the desacralizing of the water.)

CONFIRMATION AND COMMUNION

Throughout the East, anointing with oil (from the fourth century, perfumed oil, *myron*) has been substituted for signing with the cross as the sign of the seal of the Spirit. Syria seems to have been slower in doing this, perhaps because of the importance given there to the anointing *before* baptism. The older Chaldean rituals in particular apparently consider the anointing optional, and in that tradition the seal of the Spirit was conferred by laying on of hands, accompanied by a prayer in anaphora form. But by the sixteenth century the meaning of this rite was forgotten, and the Catholic Chaldeans simply took over the text from the Roman Pontifical. Western influence led the Maronites to reserve the sacrament of confirmation to the bishop, with their traditional Syrian rite; when a priest baptizes, instead of confirming as well he simply says the prayer for the postbaptismal anointing with chrism from the Roman rite. In the other rites the neophyte's naked body is anointed in numerous places (thirty-six among the Copts). The Syrian formula for anointing the forehead is: "N. is signed with holy myron, the sweet perfume of the Anointed of God [Christ God], with the seal of true faith and with the gift of the Holy Spirit, in the name of the Father and of the Son and of the holy living Spirit, unto life for ever and ever. Amen." In the Coptic rite the anointings are accompanied by various forms of words and followed by imposition of hands and a breathing, with the words: "Be blessed with the blessing of Heaven's angels. May our Lord Jesus Christ bless you. Receive the Holy Spirit. Be clean vessels through our Lord Jesus Christ, to whom be glory with his Father and the Holy Spirit, now and always." The Armenians say: "Sweet oil is poured out on you in Christ's name, as the seal of gifts from

Heaven." In the Byzantine rite, after an introductory prayer whose equivalent appears in other rites, the form is simply: "The seal of the gift of the Holy Spirit. Amen."

For centuries the making and consecrating of *myron*, chrism, has been reserved to the various patriarchs. To the oil various aromatic substances are added (fifty-seven of them in the Byzantine rite), and the long process of mixing, heating and cooling takes several days; consequently *myron* is consecreated only at long intervals. The custom of adding other ingredients no doubt originated in Egypt, the great land of perfumes. In the Chaldean rite only the Catholics use *myron*, and for long it was consecrated with the Roman-rite form for the consecration of chrism, translated into Syriac. Then, at the end of the nineteenth century, the patriarch Abdishu V Khayatt adapted the old Chaldean form of consecration of oil for the dedication of an altar, mixing a little balm with the oil. It would seem that, lacking olive oil, the Armenians and Malabarese have sometimes used other vegetable, or even animal, oils.

With the exception of the Byzantine rite, the various oriental Rituals prescribe the placing of a fillet (or "crown") on the child's head. Various prayers are said as this is done. Only the Byzantine rite has preserved some trace of the celebration of the eucharistic Liturgy at this point with the reading of the Epistle (Rom. 6. 3–11) and Gospel (Matt. 28. 16–20), followed by a litany and the communion, under the species of wine alone if the candidate is an infant. In the other rites there is only the communion. Under Latin influence the Maronites have abolished the communion of infants. Among the Chaldeans also the practice of communion at this ceremony has fallen into disuse. A short formula of dismissal, to which the Copts add the singing of a hymn, brings this long and imposing ceremony to a close.

CHAPTER VI

THE EUCHARISTIC LITURGY

The celebration of the Eucharist, the memorial of Christ's redeeming work and the sacrament of his presence in the Church, is the heart and summit of all Christian worship. Christians of the Byzantine rite call it The Holy and Divine Liturgy; for the Syrians, Armenians and Copts it is The Sacrifice (Syr. *Kurbono*; Arm. *Patarak*) or The Offering (Copt. *Prosfora*); for the Chaldeans and Ethiopians it is The Hallowing (*Kuddasha, Keddase*), sometimes The Assembly (*Synaxis*).

The variety and range of liturgies in use today at first sight obscures their inner unity of structure, which was doubtless acquired during the very first Christian generation: in the middle of the second century it was testified to by St Justin, a Palestinian, converted probably at Ephesus, who wandered all over the Mediterranean world as a teacher before he settled at Rome, where he was martyred. In his famous *Apologia*, addressed to the emperor Antoninus Pius, Justin twice describes the eucharistic liturgy, and he says nothing to suggest that it differed notably from place to place. Again, in the fourth century, pilgrims and travellers and exiles do not seem to have been at a loss when taking part in worship at places far from home. The fact is that in those days the liturgy followed practically exclusively the very simple pattern that the Christian communities of the apostolic age had received from our Lord himself, a pattern that gave new meaning to

the traditional Jewish *kiddush*: readings from the Bible inter-
spersed with the singing of psalms or hymns, a prayer of the
assembly for all man's needs, the consecratory thanksgiving
over the bread and wine (mixed with water), which was then
distributed as the "mystery" of Christ's body and blood, the
reminder of all he did to save us. This consecratory prayer
was from the first built up on the threefold pattern of the
kiddush: praise and blessing of God, the all-holy creator; recalling of his whole redeeming work as centred on the institution of the Supper; supplication and invocation (*epiklesis*)
for the complete and final fulfilment of this work by the
coming of the Kingdom.

This last part soon developed in two directions: an intercession for all members of the Church, living and dead, which
brought with it the evocation of the great forefathers who have
gone to Christ before us; and a defining of the epiclesis as a
supplication for the coming of the Spirit, who gives the sacrament its full reality and effectiveness. This second development is a characteristic of the Eastern liturgies: it is explicitly
attested in the catechetical lessons attributed to St Cyril of
Jerusalem and took a more and more important place in
the teaching of the Eastern Churches. Long before the sad
disputes between Greeks and Latins in the later Middle Ages,
the attention given to this epiclesis and the function assigned
to it gave the Eastern Eucharist a different emphasis from
that of the Latin Mass: especially the explicit stress on a
coming of the Holy Spirit to put the seal on the accomplish-
ment of the sacrament, thus underlining that the whole Trinity
is at work in it. In the West, attention is concentrated on
Christ's act of offering: the celebrant acts in Christ's name
(*in persona Christi*). In the East, after recalling what Christ
did for our salvation and the memorial that he instituted,
the celebrant humbly prays the Spirit, source of life and holiness, to make the Church's offering really to be Christ's body
and blood for those who participate in the sacrifice.

This point is specially touched on here because it is fundamental, an expression of two points of view that are different yet complementary: the same mystery of salvation is looked at and experienced under differing aspects. In the West, the presence of the one priest of the New Covenant, Jesus Christ, actualizes the redeeming sacrifice throughout time and place: it is he who acts, through the ministry of those to whom he has delegated apostolic sacramental power. In the East, the eucharistic celebration signifies and makes operative the whole economy of salvation, in which the whole Trinity is involved; and the mysterious "property" proper to each of the divine Persons is explicitly evoked.

This common basis, so soon arrived at, has been worked on by the various Eastern liturgies in diverse ways, according to the native characters of the communities concerned and the cultures that they expressed. It is now for us briefly to indicate some of these subsidiary differences by examining the various parts that have for centuries constituted the eucharistic liturgy.

PREPARATORY RITES

The earliest evidence agrees in making the eucharistic liturgy begin, after the entrance of celebrant and ministers, with readings, psalm-singing and prayers. But later on all rites introduced a formal preparation for the celebration: preparation of persons and (in nearly all rites) of the bread and wine to be offered. The preparation of persons has a double aspect: there is everywhere a preparing common to the whole assembly, but the preparing of the celebrant generally remains purely private; only the Syrians and Armenians have introduced it into the common preparatory observances.

It is only in the Byzantine rite that the preparation of the offerings is still wholly private; it is very complex and full of symbolism, and is carried out in a low voice by priest and deacon at the table of *prothesis* behind the iconostasis, whose doors are closed. In other rites it takes place at the

beginning of the celebration, and is more or less happily
adjusted to other elements in the preparation. This integration
has been done most satisfactorily in the Syrian and Maronite
rites, in the services "of Melchisedech" and "of Aaron", of
which the first centres on the preparing of the bread and wine
and the second on their offering and censing. The Armenians
have further simplified the old Byzantine *prothesis*, which was
much less complex than the present one; but the Copts have
added solemnity, by carrying the offerings in procession round
the altar before the offertory.

Whether or not it makes a frame for the above rites, the
preparation of the assembly always includes two more or less
closely associated elements: prayers and chants, and a censing of the whole church. These are found in their unspoiled
early simplicity among the Chaldeans and the Malabarese.
With them (as with the Copts) every office begins with the
Lord's Prayer; then Psalms 14, 150 and 116 are sung, and the
"anthem of the Sanctuary": "How great and glorious is your
sanctuary, O God the sanctifier of all things." This is the
prelude to the censing, which is preceded by a short prayer
of thanksgiving and accompanied by an ancient hymn that is
found in all Chaldean offices: "Lord of the universe, we praise
you; Jesus Christ, we bless you, for you give life to our bodies
and salvation to our souls." To the simplicity of the rites the
Armenians have added hymns, and private prayers for the
celebrant, whose successive actions are underlined by the
chants; while he vests, the choir sings of "the deep mystery
beyond our grasp" of God's saving dealings, which are like
a garment of light around reborn mankind. As the procession
enters the church, the choir acclaims the glory of Aaron the
priest: "Today Christ makes our celebrant appear under the
same form. As you go up to the sanctuary, remember our
dead; in the offering of the sacrifice, remember me, a sinner;
may Christ be merciful to me and to us until he comes again."
During the censing the mystery of the Church is acclaimed:
"Zion, daughter of light, mother of all, join with your children

in triumphant praise! Adorn yourself, deck yourself, majestic bride, glorious temple that shines like the heavens . . . !"

Before the censing the Copts make use of a very ancient prayer of absolution, called "the absolution of the Son", which is peculiar to the Egyptian Church; but under medieval Western influence the Armenians and Maronites introduced into the preparation a confession of sins followed by an absolution. Among the Syrians, too, the "service of Melchisedech" gives a penitential atmosphere to the preparation of the offerings; in the *sedro* of this service the choir sings: "Lord, I am knocking at your door; I am asking for mercy from your store. I am a sinner; long have I forsaken your way. Enable me to confess my misdoings, to put them behind me and live in your grace. At what door shall I knock, merciful Lord, if not at yours? Who will forgive our failings if your own mercy does not plead with you, you the King before whom kings lie prostrate?" The "service of Aaron" in the same rite joins commemoration of all members of the Church, living and dead, and intercessory prayers to the offering of the bread and wine and the censing that follows. There is the equivalent of these prayers in the three solemn "universal prayers" which are characteristic of the Coptic rite, and in the deacon's litany that opens the eucharistic liturgy of the Byzantines.

This litany is followed by a curious feature, called the *typika*, which consists of two antiphons, each followed by a very short litany. After the second antiphon is sung a hymn attributed to the emperor Justinian, which is also used by the Syrian and Armenian Churches: "Only-begotten Son and Word of God, you, being immortal, were pleased for our salvation to take flesh from the holy Mother of God, the ever-virgin Mary; without change you became man and you were crucified, O Christ our God, by death trampling down death: you who are one of the holy Trinity, glorified with the Father and the Holy Spirit, save us!"

The variety and complexity of preparatory rites are an indication of their lateness. It is sometimes the preparation of the assembly that is stressed and sometimes, less early at this point, that of the sacrificial bread and wine. The oldest recorded formula of offering comes from Egypt, the "prayer of St Mark", which has survived in the form and at the length of a consecratory anaphora. Another formula of the same type, but much shorter, given the name of St John Chrysostom, is found in the oldest Byzantine euchologies. The present formula in that rite originally belonged to the liturgy of St Basil: it is longer and less terse, and is concerned more with the hallowing of the assembly than with the offerings.

In all rites this hallowing of the assembly, and particularly of the celebrant and ministers, is the subject of prayers that are generally late and often not unlike the *apologiae sacerdotis* which were so numerous in the medieval West. The censing has everywhere been separated from the entrance procession, where no doubt it had its origin, and has become an expression of this hallowing; in several rites it is accompanied by prayers and chants of a penitential character. This is the case in the Byzantine liturgy, in which the observances have no special solemnity: after the *prothesis*, and before the Liturgy begins, the deacon censes throughout the church, saying Psalm 50 in a low voice. In other rites expression is given to a sacrifice of praise, notably with the Syrians and Maronites in the "service of Aaron", and with the Copts, who here have the three "universal prayers".

THE LITURGY OF THE WORD

Primitively, the liturgy began at once with readings, and the Roman rite has kept this on Good Friday. But soon the entrance of celebrant and ministers was given some solemnity, sometimes simply by a greeting and an opening prayer. But in Asia Minor and doubtless in Constantinople, from at least the fifth century, the procession was accompanied by a hymn: "Holy God, holy Strong One, holy Deathless One, have mercy on us." At first this hymn was certainly addressed to Christ and was a profession of faith in his divinity, and in the patriarchate of Antioch after the Council of Chalcedon this was made clear by the addition of the words "who was crucified for us". But this addition was of anti-Chalcedonian origin and the orthodox rejected it as suspect of monophysism; since then they have addressed the hymn, the *Trisagion*, to the whole Trinity.

The entrance procession has kept its early form and impressiveness at pontifical celebrations: the bishop and priests,[1] who have hitherto been in the middle of the church, advance into the sanctuary, with lights and the gospel-book. At ordinary celebrations this has given place to a solemn showing of the gospel-book at the "lesser entrance", just as the gifts are solemnly shown at the "great entrance" with which the liturgy of the faithful begins. During the singing of the Beatitudes or of the third antiphon after the *typika*, the celebrant, preceded by lights and the deacon carrying the gospel-book, leaves the sanctuary and moves across the church to the middle door of the screen; here he stops to kiss the book and say the prayer of entrance. Then the deacon exclaims: "Wisdom! Stand up!" and they re-enter the sanctuary while the choir sings: "Come, let us worship and bow down before Christ. Save us, Son of God, you who rose from the dead (*on weekdays*: you who are wonderful in your saints), we who sing to you: Alleluia!" This is followed by the singing of *troparia* proper to the day, and only then is the *Trisagion* sung, three times and very solemnly.

---

[1] The Byzantine rite has kept the ancient custom of concelebration in its fullness; even when no bishop is present several priests may concelebrate, dividing the priestly prayers between one another. Among the Catholics, all chant the words of consecration aloud together; among the Orthodox, only the principal celebrant sings them, the others joining him in a low voice, or even by simply indicating the holy gifts by a gesture of the hand. Among the Catholic Syrians, each celebrant has a separate altar and offerings, but only the senior celebrates aloud. Concelebration is more limited in the Maronite and Coptic rites. In the Chaldean rite the old usage was for a priest to be designated to present the sacrifice in the name of the bishop and assembled presbyters.

There is nothing so fine as this in any other rite. Among the Armenians the censing is followed by the entrance-chant of the day and a prayer by the celebrant, who greets the people. While the *Trisagion* is being sung, the deacon takes the gospel-book from the altar and presents it to be kissed by a representative of the congregation. Then comes the litany that the Byzantines have moved to the beginning of the celebration; this is its normal place. In the Syrian and Maronite rites the gospel-book is carried in procession round the altar while a hymn is sung, followed by the *Trisagion*. In the Syrian rite this procession should normally be preceded by three Old Testament lessons. These the Maronites have not got, but the *Trisagion* is accompanied by a censing of the altar and gifts, and the reading from St Paul follows. The Copts sing the *Trisagion* just before the gospel, so as to give the procession a more normal position. The Chaldean rite has no trace of this procession; the *Trisagion*, to the exclusion of any other hymn, comes before the Old Testament readings. But even this has disappeared from the Malabar rite, the only Eastern liturgy in which the *Trisagion* does not appear.

Some rites still retain lessons from the Old Testament: the Armenians have one, from the Prophets; the Chaldeans two, Law and Prophets; the Syrians three, Law, Wisdom and Prophets, but these have fallen out of use among the Catholics. The New Testament lessons are equally variable in number. Byzantines, Armenians, Maronites and Chaldeans have only an epistle from St Paul and a gospel, but St Paul is replaced by the Acts of the Apostles during paschaltime and, among the Byzantines, by readings from the catholic epistles during the last weeks of the liturgical year. The Syrian liturgy has a special lesson from the Acts; so too have the Copts, but among them on a saint's day it is displaced by an account of the saint, taken from the Synaxary; in the Coptic rite there is also a supplementary lesson from the catholic epistles. Usually there is a chant before the epistle, whether a *prokeimenon* from a psalm, as with the Byzantines and Maronites, or an anthem, as with the Armenians and Chaldeans. Only the Copts have no other chant than the *Trisagion* of the gospel-procession, followed by Alleluia. The solemn singing of the gospel is everywhere preceded by Alleluia, and often by a scriptural verse or a hymn.

The Malabarese and the Armenians have adopted the Roman practice of singing the Creed immediately after the gospel, whereas other rites defer it till the liturgy of the faithful. The Chaldeans sing an anthem after the gospel; Syrians, Maronites and Copts follow it with a prayer.

From the earliest times the liturgy of the word ended with a "universal prayer" for the needs of all the world, which, when there were no catechumens or other persons who were excluded from the eucharistic celebration, led straight to the sacrificial rites. In the Roman rite this prayer, after a complicated history, is now reduced to the one word "Oremus" which comes before the offertory chant. A similar thing has happened in the Maronite rite, which has now no trace of such a prayer, and in the Syrian rite it has been swallowed up in the offertory *sedro*; and it has been abolished by the Ethiopians and the Catholic Copts. The Chaldean rite has the whole of it only during Lent, but this rite has, better than others, kept the prayer "over the bowed heads" which used to end every celebration; there is an equivalent at the end of the long Armenian litany. In the Byzantine rite the deacon's litany, here as elsewhere, has smothered the priest's prayer, which is now said in a low voice, except for the last few words (*ekphonesis*). This more popular pattern allows for the detailing of the objects of petition, which are set out in a passage of the Coptic prayer; but this rite has really transferred the universal prayer to the liturgy of the faithful, in the usual Coptic threefold form.

Neither the Coptic, Syrian nor Maronite rite now contains any explicit reference to the dismissal of the catechumens and public penitents. But, though it no longer has any practical significance, this dismissal has been retained by the

Byzantines, Armenians and Chaldeans, the last in a specially impressive form. Preceded by acolytes, two ministers, one carrying a cross and the other the gospel-book, go and stand on either side of the sanctuary door, and there chant alter-nately: "Those who are not yet baptized, go out. Those who have not yet received the sign of life, go out. Whoever has not received it, go out. Levites, go and watch the doors." In the Armenian rite the deacon forbids catechumens and those whose faith is doubtful and penitents and those in sin to approach the mysteries, the singers responding with an anthem, the "hagiology", which introduces the liturgy of the faithful: "The body of the Lord and the blood of the Re-deemer are going to be made present among us. The unseen heavenly powers are singing again and again: Holy, holy, holy is the Lord God of hosts."

THE EUCHARISTIC ANAPHORA AND ITS PRELUDES

In early times the liturgy of the faithful began with the presentation of the gifts that the people had brought for the sacrifice. In most Eastern rites, as we have seen, this preparing of the bread and wine, with a first prayer of offering, now takes place at the beginning of the celebration, and from this there has resulted a certain upsetting of the first actions in the liturgy of the faithful. Thus the solemn procession with the bread and wine to the altar is now observed in its fullness only by the Byzantines and, in a less striking way, by the Armenians. The Syrians, Maronites and Chaldeans have main-tained the singing of the processional anthem but not the procession, because in the first two rites the gifts have lain ready on the altar from the beginning, and in the third they are prepared there now. At the "great entrance" of the Byzan-tine rite the majestic *Cherubikon*, Hymn of the Cherubim, is sung: "Let us who are the mystical image of the cherubim in singing the Thrice-holy Hymn to the life-giving Trinity, let us now lay aside all earthly care, that we may welcome the King of all things who draws near amidst unseen hosts of angels. Alleluia, Alleluia, Alleluia!"

In other rites the chant varies according to the feast. The Armenian "hagiologies" nearly all refer, like the *Cherubikon*, to the angelic liturgy of Heaven. The Syrians sing a hymn which links up the liturgy of the word with the eucharistic liturgy, and one at least of these has a theme very like that of the *Cherubikon*; the hymn is followed by the entrance *sedro*, which takes the place both of the "universal prayers" and of offering of incense. The Maronites have an unchanging verse, followed by a censing during the Creed. The Chaldeans sing the "anthem of the Mysteries", which varies with the feast; the text of the Sunday one is just the same as the Armenian acclamation before the hagiology. Whilst this is being sung the celebrant, having saluted the bishop and other clergy on the *bema*, prepares the bread and wine. The Catholic Chaldeans have followed the other rites in now putting this preparation at the beginning of the celebration; on the other hand, they have maintained the solemn entry of the celebrant and ministers into the sanctuary better than anyone else; this has taken place for a long time during the singing of the Creed.

This singing, or saying, of the Creed is said to have been introduced into the liturgy by a patriarch of Antioch, Peter the Fuller, at the end of the fifth century, and the practice was speedily taken up by all the Eastern Churches. While the Armenians and Malabarese have brought it forward to after the gospel, the Byzantines and Copts associate it with the kiss of peace, just before the anaphora properly so called (after the litany at the prayer of offering in the Byzantine rite).

It is a characteristic common to the Eastern liturgies that, unlike the Roman, they put the kiss of peace before the anaphora, in accordance with our Lord's words: "If thou art bringing thy gift before the altar, and rememberest there that thy brother has some ground of complaint against thee, leave thy gift lying there before the altar, and go home; be reconciled with thy brother first, and then come back to offer

thy gift" (Matt. 5. 23–4). The Armenians have carefully kept
the point of this rite, and during it they sing: "Christ showed
himself in our midst; here God, the supreme Being, has made
his dwelling-place. The voice announcing peace has sounded;
the kiss of peace has been ordained, enmity has been taken
away and charity has spread everywhere. Lift up your voices,
then, you servants of the Lord, and bless with one accord
the consubstantial and indivisible Godhead, to whom seraphim sing the hagiology." The kiss then leads directly to the
anaphora, from which in the Byzantine rite it is separated by
the Creed. In other Churches the rite is less simple. Among
Syrians, Maronites and Copts a special prayer goes with it, to
which the Chaldeans add the commemorations (diptychs)
which in the Byzantine rite occur during the great entrance.
These various liturgies also have a special prayer when the
celebrant, more or less ceremoniously, removes the veil that
covers the bread and wine; this prayer of the Veil is found
in the West in the Ambrosian rite of Milan, and it perhaps
once existed in the Roman rite.

After these preparations the anaphora[2] itself begins with
a solemn blessing, taken from St Paul: "The grace of our
Lord Jesus Christ, and the love of God, and the imparting of
the Holy Spirit be with you all" (2 Cor. 13. 13). It is followed
by the dialogue common to all Christian liturgies and used
by the Jews before them, the dialogue before the preface to
the great thanksgiving, the eucharist: "It is indeed fitting and
right to praise you and glorify you . . .". But after these opening words the text varies with each anaphora.[3] Its basic structure is the same everywhere and no doubt was, as we have
said, settled from the beginning, perhaps by our Lord himself
at the Last Supper, on the pattern of the Jewish prayers of

---

[2] *Anaphora* (Gk. offering) is equivalent to "canon of the Mass";
but it includes the preface and, in its wider acceptation, continues to
the communion. [*Trans.*]

[3] The Chaldeans alone add to the dialogue a short prayer of supplication on bended knee.

blessing and thanksgiving. The two peculiarities already mentioned are, in the Alexandrian and Roman traditions, the introduction of one or more intercessory prayers before the recital of the institution of the Eucharist; and the insertion, doubtless at a later date, of these intercessions before the anamnesis[4] and epiclesis in the Chaldean rite.

The development of the thanksgiving proper has followed two different lines. On the one hand, the blessing of the divine Name was expanded as theology progressed and new themes were elaborated by Greek thought, till it became a veritable litany. This process can be followed through a series of anaphoras of Syrian origin: that "of the Apostles" (Addai and Mari) retained in the Chaldean rite is, as we have seen, typically Semitic, while the Antiochene anaphora "of the (Twelve) Apostles" is of Greek inspiration. This last is seen to be the source of the Trinitarian developments of the Constantinopolitan anaphora that goes under the name of St John Chrysostom:

Who is able to magnify your power, Lord, to voice your praises or proclaim your wonders? Master of all things, Lord of the heavens, of the earth and of everything that is made, things visible and invisible, you sit on the throne of glory and fathom the deepest places, you who are eternal, invisible, beyond our understanding, inexpressible, unchangeable; and Father of our great God and Saviour, our Lord Jesus Christ, who is our hope, the image of your goodness, the mirror through which we see you, O Father, the living Word, true God, eternal Wisdom, Life, Holiness, Strength, true Light which revealed the Holy Spirit, Spirit of truth, Gift of adoption, Pledge of our heritage to come, First-fruits of everlasting joys, life-giving Power, Fountain of sanctification, in whose strength every rational spiritual being serves you and glorifies you in a never-ending hymn—for all creation waits upon your word. You the angels proclaim. . . .

[4] *Anamnesis* (Gk. memorial), the commemoration of Christ's passion, resurrection and ascension made after the words of institution (the prayer *Unde et memores* in the Roman rite). [*Trans.*]

The Egyptian anaphora in Serapion's prayerbook speaks the same language, with a personal accent that bears the mark of contemplation in the spirit of St John:

> We praise you, uncreated and unutterable God, beyond the understanding of all created nature. We praise you, you who are known through the sole-begotten Son, who proclaims you, interprets you and makes you known to created nature. We praise you, you who know the Son and make known his glories to those who are sanctified, you who are known through the Word whom you engendered, you who are revealed to the saints. We praise you, Father invisible, giver of immortality: source of life, source of light, source of all grace and all truth. Lover of man, lover of the poor, reconciler of all, whom you draw to yourself through the coming of your well-beloved Son. We pray you to make us living men. Give us the light-bearing Spirit that we may know you, the true [God] and him whom you have sent, Jesus Christ. Give us the Holy Spirit that we may be able to speak and tell your unutterable mysteries.

The emphasis of the other line of development is on the divine "economy", on the dispensation of the mystery of salvation in the work of creation and redemption. There is a relatively sober example of it in the Jerusalem anaphora "of St James", which begins by evoking "the heavenly Jerusalem, the company of the chosen, the church of the first-born whose names are written in Heaven, the spirits of the righteous and the prophets, the souls of the martyrs and the apostles". After this opening, which indicates its origin, and the chant of "Holy, holy, holy . . .", it goes on with the following passage, which is found almost word for word in the Alexandrian anaphora "of St Mark" and its Coptic version ("St Cyril"):

> You are holy, all-mighty, awe-inspiring, full of loving kindness and mercy. You had great goodness towards your creation: you fashioned man out of dust, in your image and likeness,

and you gave him Paradise for his portion. When he had transgressed your command and was fallen, you did not scorn and forsake him, O God of goodness; like a compassionate father, you corrected him, you appealed to him through the Law, you guided him through the Prophets. And in the fullness of time you sent into the world your own and only Son, our Lord Jesus Christ, that he might restore and give new life to your image. He came down from Heaven, took flesh from the Holy Spirit and blessed Mary, the ever-virgin Mother of God; he lived amongst men, and ordered all things for the world's salvation.

In accordance with the pattern already laid down in the anaphora of the *Apostolic Tradition*, this evocation of the saving process leads straight to the account of the eucharistic institution and the recalling of the redemptive Passion which gives the key to it. The pattern was taken up by St Basil from an older anaphora, doubtless Egyptian, and eventually we have that grand theological document, the Byzantine anaphora of St Basil: this is too long to set out here, but it ought to have a place of honour in any Christian anthology.[5] During the same era, in Antiochene Syria, the same theme led to the inordinate developments of the "Clementine Liturgy" in Book viii of the *Apostolic Constitutions*. The theme was taken up in all the Syrian, Armenian and Ethiopian anaphoras deriving from those "of St James" and of St Basil, but they did not succeed in safeguarding the perfect balance of the original arrangement.

Apart from these two types, "theologic" and "economic", a few Syrian and Ethiopian anaphoras used different, secondary themes. Mention may be made of the Coptic anaphora "of St Gregory the Theologian" (of Nazianzus), which is un-

[5] According to the most recent studies of Dom Bernard Capelle, the "Egyptian" form of the anaphora could itself represent a first version by St Basil. [There is an English version of the Byzantine St Basil in *The Orthodox Liturgy*, ed. Patrick Thompson (London, 1939) and in Englert (see Bibliography herein), as well as in several older standard works. *Trans.*]

usual in being addressed directly to the Son,[6] and of the more recent Ethiopian anaphora "of the holy Virgin Mary".

Whatever precedes and introduces it, the heart of any eucharistic anaphora is the recital of the institution of the Eucharist at the Last Supper. With very rare exceptions, Eastern liturgies, unlike those of the West, put this institution "in the night when the Lord was betrayed", as St Paul does (1 Cor. 11. 23). More surprising is the fact that the Chaldean anaphora "of the Apostles" and a few Syrian ones leave out this recital altogether. There has been much discussion about this, in the course of which some rather wild theories have been concocted, as well as more likely ones. But it seems that in fact this omission was made only in the written texts, that these most holy words were not written down at first for fear the text should be profaned—a scrupulous care quite in line with Judaic ideas. After extensive study, Dom Bernard Botte[7] thinks there is every likelihood that originally this anaphora had a recital of the institution, and that one can get an idea of it from that in the anaphora called "of Theodore of Mopsuestia" which is a rearrangement of it: Jesus, "in the night when he was betrayed, celebrated this great, this awe-inspiring, holy and divine mystery with his apostles. Taking bread, he blessed it, broke it, gave it to his disciples and said: This is my body which is broken for you, for the forgiveness of sins. The same with the cup: he gave thanks, and gave it to them and said: This is my blood of the new covenant, which is shed for the multitude for the forgiveness of sins. So take, all of you, and eat this bread and drink of this cup, and do the same every time you meet together in memory of me." Behind its many variants and elaborations in the different

[6] Though it has been preserved only in Egypt, this anaphora is of Syrian origin; it was used principally by the monks in the desert of Skete, where there was an important monastery dedicated in honour of our Lady. At the present time this anaphora is used in the Easter liturgy on Holy Saturday night.

[7] *Op. cit.*, p. 38.

liturgies the recital is fundamentally the same, the foundation-stone and core of the whole eucharistic celebration.

But it must be clearly recognized that the words of institution do not have the dominant place in Eastern instruction and piety that they have in the Western tradition. We have already had occasion to notice this difference, which is not necessarily a disagreement (cf. pp. 76–7). It is a fact that from at least the fourth century the invocation, epiclesis, which is found in various forms in all liturgies (it is not missing from the Roman Mass[8]), took on an ever-increasing importance, as more clearly expressing the Holy Spirit's part in the sacrificial gifts' becoming the Lord's body and blood for those who receive them. The progress of this clarification and of the more and more precise meaning given to the Holy Spirit's intervention can be followed through the still-available textual documents. In the anaphora of Hippolytus the celebrant prays: "Send your Holy Spirit upon the holy Church's offering, to gather into one all the holy people who partake." The epiclesis of the Chaldean anaphora "of the Apostles" would seem to be a later addition to a text that did not call for it: it is still close to the meaning that it had for Hippolytus, asking simply that: "May your Holy Spirit come and rest on this your servants' offering, may he bless it and hallow it, that it may be for us, Lord, atonement for our misdoings and forgiveness for our sins, in the great hope of resurrection from the dead and of new life in the kingdom of Heaven with all who have been found acceptable in your sight." The same idea is found in the earliest form of St Basil's anaphora, in which the Chaldean formula perhaps originated. In all these cases the object of the epiclesis is to ask for the coming of the Holy Spirit on the gifts so that the meaning of the offering may be fulfilled.

---

[8] The prayers *Supplices te rogamus*, after the consecration and anamnesis, and *Quam oblationem*, before the consecration, represent epicleses of the archaic type that does not explicitly express the invocation of the Holy Spirit.

But from the middle of the fourth century a new clarification appears, as may be seen in St Cyril's catechetical instructions, in the Clementine liturgy of the *Apostolic Constitutions*
and especially in the oldest form of the anaphora "of St
James": it is explicitly asked that the Spirit may be sent to
make the bread Christ's body and the wine his blood. This
idea was gradually extended to most of the Eastern anaphoras,
and it finds its best expression in the Byzantine Liturgy of
St John Chrysostom: "We pray you, we beseech you, we
implore you to send down your Holy Spirit on us and on these
gifts here. And make this bread the precious body of your
Christ, and that which is in this cup the precious blood of
your Christ, changing them by your Holy Spirit." The prayer
is often emphasized by a prostration of the celebrant and
ministers. In certain Churches of Byzantine rite in recent times
a threefold repetition of a *troparion* from the office of Pentecost has been inserted into the traditional epiclesis; this
interpolation is perhaps not free from anti-Roman significance.

In most rites the epiclesis is followed by intercessions for
the living and the dead. The only exceptions are the Alexandrian "St Mark", which has the intercessions in the first
part of the anaphora, and the Chaldean liturgy, which puts
them before the epiclesis or even, in the anaphora "of the
Apostles", before the anamnesis. But the anaphora proper
everywhere concludes with a more or less elaborated
Trinitarian doxology.

THE BREAKING OF THE BREAD, COMMUNION
AND THANKSGIVING

The last part of the eucharistic liturgy is made up of several
rites, arranged differently according to the liturgy concerned;
there are nevertheless several main points common to all.
The Lord's Prayer is preceded (except among the Copts) by
an introductory prayer and followed (except among the

Byzantines) by the embolism, that is, an elaboration of the last petition.[9] The consecrated Bread is broken before the Lord's Prayer in the Syrian, Chaldean and Coptic rites, after it among the Byzantines, Armenians and Maronites. The associated rites of showing the holy Gifts and of the commixture or the intinction[10] of the sacramental elements occur at various places. The showing of the Gifts, with the words "Holy things to holy people", always comes after the prayer of blessing "over the bowed heads", which follows the embolism of the Lord's Prayer. The commixture or consignation-intinction normally goes with the breaking of the Bread, but not among the Copts, who have the breaking before the Lord's Prayer and the other observances after the showing of the Gifts.

Particular points worth noting are the litanies before the Lord's Prayer in the Byzantine and Armenian rites and—corresponding to them—the "universal prayers", or the hymn that replaces them, among the Syrians, Maronites and Chaldeans. With the Copts these prayers are more like a new series of commemorations, and their place is just before the showing of the Gifts. They are preceded by a specially striking prayer called the "absolution of the Father", which in turn follows the prayer over the bowed heads, called by the Copts the prayer of St Mark. The "absolution of the Father" quotes our Lord's promise to St Peter and the Church, the power of binding and loosing, and goes on to ask for celebrant and people forgiveness for past sins and grace that they may not fall again. The Gifts are shown in specially solemn form in the Armenian, Syrian and Maronite rites; in the first case probably, and in the last possibly, this is in part due to

[9] A form of the conclusion, so familiar in England and elsewhere, "For thine is the kingdom, the power and glory, for ever and ever", is said at the end of the Lord's Prayer in most Eastern liturgies. [*Trans.*]
[10] *Commixture* is the dropping of a small piece of the Bread into the chalice; *intinction* is the marking of the Bread with a drop of the Wine, which may be done in the form of a cross (*consignation*).

influence from the later medieval West, which attached so much importance to the elevation of the Host. But in all Eastern rites the significance of this showing is indicated by the words which precede or accompany it, "Holy things to holy people"; the congregation responds by an expression of faith in the Trinity and in Christ which makes a good preparation for communion.

Holy communion is received standing and under both kinds, except among the Catholic Armenians, Maronites and Malabarese. In the Coptic and the old Chaldean rites the communicant receives each kind separately; Byzantines and Syrians are given the species of bread immersed in or moistened with the species of wine. Before and after communion the holy Things are solemnly offered for the people's worship. Except in the Chaldean rite, communion is now preceded by prayers and professions of faith of more or less recent composition; the celebrant says them in a loud voice so that all may associate themselves with them, and in Byzantine usage he repeats them for the benefit of lay communicants; the traditional communion chant is generally anticipated before these prayers. After communion and a blessing with the Gifts (unknown in the Chaldean and Coptic rites) there is a thanksgiving, always consisting of a prayer, an exhortation and another prayer that ends with a blessing. Chaldean and Coptic congregations then say the Lord's Prayer. Except among the Syrians, the dismissal is accompanied by a final blessing with the cross, and among the Copts the people are sprinkled with the water with which the celebrant has rinsed his hands. Before leaving the church, Byzantines and Armenians come and kiss the cross and the hand of the celebrant who holds it, and receive a piece of *antidoron*, bread from which the portions to be consecrated were cut.

The Syrian and Maronite celebrant before he leaves the sanctuary takes a solemn farewell of the altar:

> Remain in peace, holy altar of the Lord; I know not if I shall again return to you or no. May the Lord grant that I

shall see you amidst the assembly of the first-born in Heaven: in that covenant I put my trust. Remain in peace, holy and atoning altar: may the holy Body and the atoning Blood that I have received from you be for the forgiveness of my misdoings, the remission of my sins and my safeguard when I stand before the judgement-seat of our Lord, the ever-living God. Remain in peace, holy altar, table of life, pleading for me before our Lord Jesus Christ that I may always have him in mind, henceforth and for ever. Amen.

CHAPTER VII

THE RITES OF PENITENCE, OF SICKNESS AND OF DEATH

It is easier in Eastern liturgies than in the Roman liturgy to comprise in a single examination those rites (of unequal importance) which have in common that they are addressed to man as sinner and suffering from the consequences of sin, sickness and death. The two fundamental sacraments of baptism and the eucharist received their essential rites from our Lord himself, and from the earliest times they grew into a liturgy which is substantially identical everywhere; but we now have to touch on matters which received their full doctrinal and liturgical expression in the Church much more slowly. It was not until the twelfth and thirteenth centuries that clear doctrine about the sacraments of penitence and anointing of the sick emerges, first in the West and then in most of the Eastern Churches, partly under the influence of Latin theology; the Nestorian Church of the East Syrians seems never to have attained it. This Church included funeral rites among the "mysteries", alongside monastic dedication and the consecration of altars; but it does not appear to have known sacramental rites either for the forgiveness of sin or anointing of the sick. In the other Churches this last requirement gave rise to a ritual which to a considerable extent they have in common: the "rite of the lamp", very different from that which was formed in the West during the high Middle Ages. But with the rites of repentance it is otherwise: their forms vary too much from Church to Church for us to be able to assign a very great age to them. Nevertheless in nearly every case there can be recognized an adaptation and extension of rites which originated in the reconciliation of apostates or of public sinners who had had to be temporarily excluded from the Church.

SACRAMENTAL CONFESSION AND ABSOLUTION

The Nestorian Church had only the rite of reconciliation. The form attributed to the catholicos Ishu'yab III was intended in the first place for the reconciliation of apostates and heretics, but its use was extended to public sinners. It took place before the communion in the eucharistic Liturgy. For the previous three days the penitent had sat in sackcloth and ashes outside the door of the sanctuary, head and feet bare, his girdle round his neck. After the Lord's Prayer and the singing of Psalms 122 and 129, antiphons and hymns, the priest laid his hands on the penitent's head, saying a prayer of reconciliation for which several texts were provided; finally there was a signing with the cross, and sometimes an anointing. This solemn observance seems to have fallen into disuse a long time ago, and the Catholic Chaldeans simply use the Roman ritual of penance, translated into Syriac.

With much less reason, this practice was imposed on the Catholic Syrians by the Council of Sharfeh in 1888. But in fact, unlike the East Syrians, the Church of Antioch at an early date had a solid theology of sacramental penance, and in its liturgy there are several formulas that answer perfectly to the requirements of the Catholic faith in this respect. The most important of them is attributed to the great theologian Dionysius bar Salibi; he was a contemporary and friend of the twelfth-century patriarch Michael the Great who was responsible for the Syrian Pontifical, and this book includes a careful description of the rite of confession.

It first sets out the obligations that bind the confessor: not to reveal anything he has learned in confession, not to make the penitent feel embarrassed subsequently, and to be careful not to discourage him, and not to show "respect for persons". Then it directs that confessions shall be heard at the church door or in the sanctuary. The penitent, kneeling bareheaded, face turned to the ground and arms crossed, accuses himself to the priest who sits close by. Then priest and penitent say together a number of hymns, psalms and prayers calculated to excite sorrow for sin. At any rate in principle, all Eastern Churches have maintained the old tradition that the whole community of the faithful ought to join in the penitent's prayers for God's mercy, and to give him moral support in his efforts to be a true returned prodigal son before his Father in Heaven. A too juridical approach often makes us in the West forget that the sacrament of penance is the highest expression of the virtue of penitence, and that this is not simply a personal thing but calls for the cooperation of the Christian community. The long supplication is followed by imposition of a satisfaction, "giving a penance", generally in the form of fasting or some other bodily mortification or of almsgiving. Only after this penance has been done does the penitent receive absolution, properly speaking. The Syrian Church, which has a number of deprecatory formulas having reference to different sins, seems to reserve for the absolution proper the following form, which is accompanied by imposition of hands, a breathing and a triple sign of the cross: "Sin is taken away from your soul and your body in the name of the Father, Amen. You are then made clean and holy in the name of the Son. Amen. May you be forgiven and share in the holy mysteries in the name of the Holy Spirit (for everlasting life). Amen."

The Churches of Byzantine rite, whether Catholic or Orthodox, have a ritual of the same type, but noticeably shorter. It explicitly provides that all the prayers, which in this case precede the confession of sins, should be said by the whole group of penitents together; each individual in turn then approaches the priest, who sits or stands by an icon, generally in front of the iconostasis. Especially among the Slavs, it is customary for the penitent to stand beside the priest, who lays the end of his stole on the penitent's head, at least while absolution is given. But confession may be made sitting, facing the priest, and this tends to be the usage in Greece today. There is a choice of several formulas of absolution; the Slavs alone use an active form as in the Latin West ("I absolve you. . . ."). Among the Greek Orthodox the confessor is still at liberty to compose his own formula of absolution, but the one generally used since at least the eleventh century is: "Lord our God, you remitted the sins of Peter and of the harlot [Luke 7. 37] because of their tears, and justified the publican who acknowledged his own sinfulness [ib., 18. 10–14]: accept then the confession of this your servant; if he has committed any sins, voluntarily or involuntarily, in word, deed or thought, in your goodness forgive him, for you alone have the power to remit sin, you who are the God of compassion, of mercy and of love for mankind, to whom we give glory, with your eternal Father and with the holy, good and life-giving Spirit, now and always and for ever. Amen."

At least among the Orthodox, absolution is not given until after the *epitimion* (satisfaction) has been done; this is often very severe and long, in accordance with the still authoritative medieval Penitential attributed to the patriarch John the Faster. A consequence of this excessive severity is that confession is infrequent, involving a corresponding infrequency of holy communion.

The Armenians seem to have adopted a shorter and simpler ritual at a fairly early date: it is ascribed to the catholicos Mashdots, who reorganized their liturgy in the ninth century. But its present form shows signs of strong Latin influence and cannot be dated earlier than the crusades; it is not attested before the twelfth century. The penitent, kneeling beside the confessor, listens to or says a long form of general confession;

then he accuses himself of his sins, and the priest, stretching out his hand, says:

> May the very compassionate God have mercy on you and grant remission of all the sins you have confessed and of those which you have forgotten. And in virtue of my priesthood, by the authority and at the order of God expressed in the words "All that you shall loose on earth shall be loosed in Heaven", I absolve you from every bond of sin, thoughts, words and deeds, in the name of the Father and of the Son and of the Holy Spirit, and I restore you to the sacraments of the holy Church. May all the good that you do increase your merit and add to your glory in the life to come. Amen.

There is often added:

> The shedding of the blood of God's Son on the cross freed humankind from Hell, and it is that which frees you from your sins. Amen.

As among the Syrians, there are formulas appropriate to different sins. The practice of collective confession, at any rate for children, has been kept up by the dissident Armenians: after the preparatory prayers the priest reads out a long list of faults, and each child is invited to strike his breast unobtrusively, at those of which he feels guilty.

Finally, in the Coptic Church, teaching and use of the sacrament of penitence dropped into the background for a long time, probably because of the difficulty of free access to a priest after the establishment of the Fatimid empire in 969. Traditional teaching was restored through the personal intervention of the Syrian patriarch Michael the Great, who rectified the erroneous theories of the Coptic bishop Michael of Damietta. But in practice (except among the Catholics) it still remains too common to confess "to the thurible", that is, by recalling one's sins during the censing at the beginning of the eucharistic Liturgy, which is generally looked on as a purification rite. It is in fact followed in the Coptic rite by a solemn form of absolution, called "the absolution of the Son", which in Catholic ritual is used for sacramental absolution. The first part of this fine prayer is deprecative, imploring Christ's forgiveness in virtue of his promises to the apostles; the second part is an invocation, asking that absolution may be given "from the mouth of the All-holy Trinity . . . , from the mouth of the one, holy, catholic, apostolic Church of God", from the mouths of the Twelve Apostles, of the great Doctors, of the Fathers of the ecumenical councils and of the ecclesiastical hierarchy. Another but less explicit formula of absolution, called "of the Father", is said before the communion.

ANOINTING OF THE SICK; FUNERALS

"Is one of you sick? Let him send for the presbyters of the church, and let them pray over him, anointing him with oil in the Lord's name. Prayer offered in faith will restore the sick man, and the Lord will give him relief; if he is guilty of sins, they will be pardoned" (James 5. 14–15). This injunction was faithfully followed in the Church, and the oldest liturgical and canonical documents have a form for blessing the oil of the sick. However, the relevant sacramental rites appear to have been slow in forming. The East Syrian Church, whose archaism we have remarked several times, does not seem to have recognized the sacramental value of oil blessed for the sick, whether used for anointing or drinking. At one time it attached importance to anointing *the dead*, a custom perhaps borrowed from Antiochene Syria, but for the sick preference was given to *'henana*, "holy dust", gathered from martyrs' graves and mixed with oil and water into pills, which were blessed by an invocation of the apostle Thomas. Apparently this was never looked on as more than a pious practice, certainly not as a sacrament. The Catholic Chaldeans of today have the rite of anointing the sick according to the Roman Ritual, translated into Syriac; but the oil is blessed with an ancient local formula.

In all the other Eastern Churches this anointing is a very solemn office, whose length and complexity unfortunately rather restricts its use; in some rites, shorter offices tend to be adopted, at any rate among the Catholics. Under the variations proper to each Church a common basis is easily detected, expressed in the name so widely used, "the rite of the lamp": the anointings are done with the oil, blessed, used in church lamps. The presence of a number of priests, generally seven, is normally required.

Take, for example, the Byzantine ritual. It presupposes that the sacrament is ministered in church, before a gathering of the faithful; but if the sick person cannot be taken there, two or three priests go to the sick-room. The rite has three parts: an "office of comfort" (Greek *parakletike*; Slavonic *moleben*), modelled on the morning office, as is used on very varied other occasions; the blessing of the oil; the anointings.

The *kanon* of the office hymns the healing power of oil and invokes God's mercy on the invalid. Between the final verses of the psalms of Lauds it is customary to interpolate *troparia* of supplication. The oil is blessed in common by all the priests present, and this too is accompanied by *troparia*, in honour of the two apostles James, of St Nicholas of Myra, of St Demetrius the Great Martyr, of the Holy Physicians who took no fees, of St John the Apostle and of the Virgin Mary. There are seven anointings, each accompanied by a long prayer, with an epistle and a gospel before each; as in the eucharistic Liturgy, each reading is preceded by psalm verses and alleluias. At the end of the rite the gospel-book is laid on the sick man's head, while the senior priest prays for the forgiveness of his sins. All these texts are distinctly penitential; the emphasis changes smoothly from bodily sickness to the sin of which sickness is a direct or indirect consequence, and from physical suffering patiently borne to atonement and expiation for wrongdoing.

The length and fullness of this office consort uneasily with the state of one who is seriously ill; but it is very impressive, and we can see how it came to be used as a penitential office, especially when we remember that, as has already been said, the reconciliation of penitents was sometimes accompanied by a signing or anointing. Accordingly, the Greek Church long ago introduced the custom of celebrating the office of Holy Oil during penitential seasons and especially in Holy Week. To avoid the grave ambiguity that could arise when they celebrate this office on Easter day, the Catholic Melkites then leave out the solemn prayer said at each anointing, which constitutes the form of the sacrament of the sick in the strict sense: "Holy Father, physician of souls and bodies, you sent your only-begotten Son, Jesus Christ, to heal every evil and deliver us from death: cure then this servant of yours of his weakness of body and soul by the grace of your Christ. Preserve this man's life, and at your good pleasure he will by good works render you the thanks that he owes. . . ." (The intercession of a number of saints is then invoked.) In Russia this anointing of people in good health took place only on Maundy Thursday, and only in the cathedral of the Assumption at Moscow and in the church of the monastery of the Holy Trinity and St Sergius. There the ritual was adapted in such a way as to get rid of all ambiguity; there was only one anointing, right at the end of the service, with the words: "The blessing of the Lord God and Saviour Jesus Christ for the welfare of the soul and body of God's servant N., now and always and for ever. Amen."

Since the Middle Ages the Syrians have a solemn blessing of oil of the sick by the bishop on Maundy Thursday; the Catholics use no other. But the Office of the Lamp really consists of five complete offices, each comprising an opening prayer, Psalm 50, hymns, prayers, anthems, epistles, gospels and litanies, and ending with the anointing of an organ of sense. For sacramental form the Catholics use an ancient absolution, to which four words have been added to make its new purpose clear: "May you be restored to health and cleansed from your sins by this holy anointing. May every evil thought be dispelled and driven away, in the name of the Father and of the Son and of the Holy Spirit, for ever-lasting life. Amen." This adoption is another example of the "give-and-take" between penitential rites and the anointing of the sick.

The Coptic and Armenian anointing rituals are very like the Byzantine in their second and third parts; the preparatory part is, of course, in accordance with the usages of each rite. But among the dissident Armenians this sacrament has for long fallen into disuse.

It is natural that *funeral* customs should vary a great deal, for they are not governed by rules imposed by an ancient tradition. Unlike those of the Roman rite, there is a certain opulence about them, incorporating elements ultimately taken over from pre-christian sources, varying from place to place. It has been remarked that several of them, including the Byzantine, retain traces of a final anointing, and the same rite has two touching observances of its own: the kissing of the body before burial and the written absolution put in its hand. But in one form or another a final absolution is found everywhere, and it certainly looks as if it is a fundamental element in Christian funeral ritual. The "absolution of the Son", whose importance is mentioned above, is said at Coptic funerals. Equally general, under diverse forms, are traces of a former vigil ("wake") with bible-readings, psalmody, hymns and prayers. There is usually a ritual proper to each category of the faithful—man, woman, child, clergy of differing orders, monks. Peculiar to the Chaldeans is the office of comfort on the two days following burial: this is the complement of the office of congratulation that follows birth.

CHAPTER VIII

THE RITES OF ORDINATION

Like those of initiation and of the Eucharist, the rites for ordaining the Church's ministers belong to the oldest level of Christian liturgy. In the course of ages they underwent such diverse and extensive developments that their original form at times became blurred. This happened in the Roman rite from the twelfth century and eventually brought forth the constitution *Sacramentum ordinis* of Pope Pius XII in 1947. The expressive rites of the delivery (*porrectio*) of the articles that characterize the duties of each order, and of the anointing of the bishop's and priest's hands, had pushed into the background the laying on of hands that accompanies the great consecratory prayer. But it is precisely this which is alone common to all liturgies and attested in the oldest documents; and Pius XII solemnly confirmed that imposition of hands is the essential rite in the ordination of bishops, priests and deacons, the three orders that formally constitute the Christian hierarchy.

In a general way the Eastern Churches have remained more consistently faithful to this primitive practice. The Armenian Church, however, has adopted Western practice both in the institution of various lesser ministries and in the ordination rites; but these meaningful developments do not obscure the essential rite.

Particular mention may be made of a remarkable formula

that is found, with tiny variations, in all Eastern rites of ordination to the three sacred orders. It seems to be kept in its earliest purity by the Byzantines, who use it for appointment to the episcopate, priesthood and diaconate alike; in other rites it is in general conserved best for the episcopate. The Byzantine formula is: "Divine grace, which ever gives strength to weakness and supplies what is lacking, chooses N. as bishop [priest, deacon]. Let us then pray for him, that the grace of the Holy Spirit may come upon him."

There has been a lot of discussion about the sacramental value of this formula, which in the Antiochene and Coptic rites is today no more than a declaration by the archdeacon; but in the other rites it is said by the ordaining bishop, sometimes, it is true, before the laying on of hands. Its universal use in the East is impressive, and so is the fact that it can be traced from the fourth century in the patriarchate of Antioch.[1] It looks as if we must see the form of the sacrament in it, at any rate in the Syrian tradition and the rites derived therefrom[2]; the more so since these conclusions of a more elaborated theology can be found at so early a date. If it be so, it is to be remarked that for the sacrament of orders, as for baptism and the eucharistic institution, a declarative form is preferred to one of petition (epiclesis), which comes in only as complementary.

Nevertheless, the formula itself requires such a complement. In the oldest evidence, that of Pseudo-Dionysius and

[1] See Dom. B. Botte's study of the whole question in *L'Orient Syrien*, II (Paris, 1957), pp. 285–297.

[2] Such is the opinion of the great Greek theologian Simeon of Thessalonica (d. 1429); writing of ordination to the diaconate he says: "When the bishop says 'as deacon', he who is ordaining confers the gift of grace and he who is ordained receives the diaconate through the hierarch's word, at once. For the word is made effective by the holy and divine Spirit, because the bishop does not speak as a man but as a hierarch, with grace; the grace is produced and is operative, since God's word is effective and one and the same Spirit does all." (*De sacris ordinibus*, ch. 149; Migne, *Patrologia Graeca*, 155, col. 377).

of the Byzantine ritual for episcopal consecration in MS. Barberini 336 (eighth century), "Divine grace..." is said during the laying on of hands; but nowadays, in every rite, there is an epiclesis at this point, as in the very old rite described in the *Apostolic Tradition* of Hippolytus. This valuable document must be studied closely. If it is connected in origin with Roman and perhaps Alexandrian usages, it was adopted and adapted in numerous versions, not only Egyptian but, even more, Syrian. The first[3] show no notable development, but in the neighbourhood of Antioch at the end of the fourth century the compiler of the *Apostolic Constitutions* adapted it to Syrian customs. Probably a little later, and in all likelihood farther into the interior of Syria, the *Testamentum Domini* provides a new adaptation; it is still fuller, and illustrates that current towards a monastic conception of ecclesiastical life that strongly characterizes later Syrian tradition. Now at least one formula, that of episcopal consecration, passed in this last form into the Pontifical of the Antiochene Church, for the consecration of the patriarch. But most of the themes of the different formulas composed in various rites are already found in the ritual of Hippolytus.

EPISCOPAL CONSECRATION

The *Apostolic Tradition* says:

That man shall be ordained bishop who has been chosen by all the people. When he has been named and approved by everybody, the people shall assemble on the Lord's day with the college of presbyters and those bishops who are at hand. With the consent of all, the bishops shall lay their hands upon him, the priests standing by quietly. Everybody shall keep silent, praying in their hearts for the coming down of the Spirit. At the request of the rest, one of the bishops, laying his

[3] *Arabic Canons of Hippolytus* (probably mid-fourth century) and *Egyptian* and *Ethiopian Canons of the Apostles* (often called the "Egyptian Church Order").

hand on him who is being ordained bishop, shall pray, saying
as follows:

"God and Father of our Lord Jesus Christ, Father of mercies
and God of all consolation, you who live on high and have
care for the lowly, you know all things before they come to
pass, you have fixed the order of your Church by the word
of your grace, from all eternity predestining the holy race
sprung from Abraham; you have made leaders and priests,
not leaving your holy place without a ministry, and from
the beginning of the world you have been pleased to be glorified by those whom you have chosen. Pour forth now the
power that comes from you, the sovereign Spirit which you
gave to your beloved Son Jesus Christ, which he bestowed on
the holy apostles who established your Church in your holy
place for the unfailing praise and glory of your name. Father,
searcher of hearts, grant that your servant, whom you have
chosen to be a bishop, may feed your holy flock and exercise
your high-priesthood without reproach, serving you day and
night; that he may ever draw down your mercy and offer up
your holy Church's gifts; that he may have power to remit
sin in virtue of the Spirit of high-priesthood, as you have commanded, that he may assign portions according to your dis-
position, that he may loose every bond by the authority that
you gave to the apostles; that he may please you by gentleness
and cleanness of heart, offering you a sweet fragrance through
your servant Jesus Christ our Lord, through whom be to you
glory, power and honour, Father and Son, with the Holy
Spirit (in the holy Church), now and always and for ever.
Amen."

The *Apostolic Constitutions* (bk. viii, ch. 4) repeat the
decisions of the fourth-century councils concerning the addition of two episcopal coconsecrators, but as a general rule the
ordination formulas, and sometimes even the imposition of
hands, are reserved to the principal consecrator. In the same
document there appears the practice of resting the gospel-book
on the head or shoulders of the bishop elect during his consecration. This observance spread throughout the Church,

except that among the Copts the book is simply laid on the
new bishop's breast at the end of the rite.

It soon came about that a bishop had to make an explicit
profession of faith at his consecration. The Armenians follow
Roman custom and proceed by way of question and answer;
otherwise the bishop elect reads a prescribed form, which in
some rites must be written out by his own hand. To these
common elements must be added the solemn declaration of
election by the formula "Divine grace . . ." (above) and the
delivery of various episcopal insignia; apart from these
matters, the rites differ very considerably from one church
to another. Among the Armenians, "Divine grace . . ." is said
during the imposition of the gospel-book, and the anointing
of head and thumbs while Psalm 132 is sung has been introduced from the Roman rite. The Syrians and Maronites carry
out episcopal consecration (and other ordination) at the end
of the eucharistic anaphora. This is to enable the consecrator,
before laying on his hands, to touch the sacred Elements three
times, as if to signify that it is from immediate contact with
Christ that he draws the graces he is about to communicate
to the bishop elect. This essential part is preceded by a long
series of chants, readings and prayers which stress the apostolic character of the episcopate, naming its requirements and
duties. In the Maronite ritual the imposition of hands is
repeated three times, and there is an anointing of head and
hands (taken from Roman practice.)

The Chaldean ceremony begins on the previous evening
with a vigil office; this is wholly given up to acclaiming the
apostolic character of the episcopate, which is perhaps nowhere better emphasized than in this Church. The same theme
is repeated in the hymns at the eucharistic Liturgy; afterwards
the gospel-book is laid on the bishop-elect's shoulders and
passages read therefrom, including Matthew 16. 13–19 (Peter's
confession) and John 21. 15–17 (Peter's pastoral responsibility).
The formula "Divine grace . . ." is given its full weight, being
said during the first of two impositions of hands. The

Byzantine and Coptic rituals are simpler, particularly the latter. This consists of a profession of faith, an introductory prayer common to all ordinations, and the proclamation "Divine grace . . . " by the archdeacon; a short epiclesis accompanies the laying on of hands; the pastoral staff is delivered and the gospel book laid on the new bishop's breast; and finally the consecrator addresses a brief admonition to him. In the Byzantine rite the pastoral staff is given immediately after the three-fold profession of faith, at the "little entrance"; ordination properly so called is conferred after the *Trisagion* and it has two prayers of petition, during the second of which one of the assisting bishops intones a litany to which the others respond; then the new bishop is vested with the episcopal stole (*omophorion*) and greeted with the acclamation "He is worthy!"

ORDINATION OF PRIESTS

In the *Apostolic Tradition* the rôle of priests seems modest enough; they appear principally to form the council that helps the bishop in the different duties of his ministry. The rite for celebrating the Eucharist is immediately associated with that of episcopal consecration, while the ordination of priests is described only afterwards, briefly and simply, as follows:

When a man is ordained priest, the bishop shall lay his hand on his head, while the priests also touch him. And the bishop shall pray, using words similar to those said above in the case of a bishop, saying:

"God and Father of our Lord Jesus Christ, look on this your servant and bestow on him the Spirit of grace and counsel of the priesthood, that he may sustain and direct your people with a pure heart, as you looked on your chosen people and commanded Moses to choose elders whom you filled with the Spirit given to your servant. And now, Lord, grant that the Spirit of your grace may always be preserved amongst us, and make us worthy to serve you with faith in simplicity of heart, praising you through your servant Christ Jesus, through whom be to you, Father and Son, with the Holy Spirit, glory and might in the holy Church, now and always and for ever. Amen."

The *Canons of Hippolytus* do not reproduce this prayer. Interpreting the preliminary rubric strictly, they prescribe the same prayer for the ordination of a priest as for that of a bishop, only changing the name of the office. They forbid the priest to sit in the episcopal chair (*cathedra*) and refuse him power to ordain: but for the rest they put him in the same position as a bishop. Further on they recognize explicitly that communities too small to have a bishop at their head will be put in charge of a priest, both for government and for ministration of the sacraments. So probably from the middle of the fourth century the need was felt of clarifying the priest's powers and the extent of his participation in the bishop's priesthood. In the Roman rite the consecratory prayer for the ordination of a priest follows the same line, but it is amplified by other prayers and observances.

It was the same in the East. Developing the text of Hippolytus, the *Apostolic Constitutions*, evidence of Antiochene usage at the end of the fourth century, ask that the priest may be filled with grace so that in carrying out his sacred duties he may fulfil a healing and teaching ministry (bk viii, ch. 16). The *Testamentum Domini* (bk i, ch. 30) is still more explicit: in a passage that is pretty close to the one that now figures in the admonition to candidates for priesthood in the Roman rite, it says that the priest blesses, preaches, celebrates the Eucharist and the office of praise.

In the various priestly ordination rituals of the East there are the same common features and the same peculiarities as in those for bishops. That of the Byzantines is notably sober: after the "great entrance" the candidate kneels, with forehead and hands resting on the altar; the bishop says "Divine grace ..." (page 106), blesses him thrice, and lays his hand on his head while saying two prayers in a low voice; during the second of these the archdeacon leads a litany. Finally, the new priest is vested, whilst "He is worthy!" is sung thrice, and he then concelebrates the eucharistic Liturgy.

It has been explained above that in the Syrian and Maronite rites ordination takes place at the end of the anaphora, so that the bishop can touch the consecrated Elements before he lays on hands. The prayer of priestly ordination, like the one before it, sets out the priest's powers fully, notably that of offering the eucharistic sacrifice; they also stress (taking their cue from the readings from the gospels and St Paul) the corporate and apostolic character of Christian priesthood. The Maronites, prolix as usual, repeat the imposition of hands three times and add an anointing of the ordinand's hands in the Roman manner. The emphasis of the Chaldean rite is on the priest as minister of the sanctuary and deputy in divine service; but it also details the various activities of the priestly ministry and the hierarchical distribution of the Christian priesthood. The same care is found in the Coptic rite, and the Armenians have shown it by taking over from the Roman ritual the delivery of chalice and paten and the anointing of the ordinand's hands. Thus we find that the extent and limits of the liturgical functions proper to the priest are everywhere clearly expressed; his rôle as immediate collaborator with the bishop is less generally brought out. Here once again the Roman rite is nearer to the oldest tradition.

ORDINATION OF DEACONS

When compared with what it says about priests, the attention and fullness of the *Apostolic Tradition*'s passage about deacons is striking. It runs thus:

> At the ordination of a deacon, he is chosen according to what has been said above, the bishop alone laying his hands on him. We direct that only the bishop should do this in the case of a deacon because he is not being ordained to the priesthood, but to serve the bishop and do his bidding. He does not take part in the council of the clergy; he has his own duties to attend to, and makes known to the bishop what needs to be

done. He does not receive the Spirit of the college of presbyters, in which the priests share, but simply [does] what the bishop entrusts to him. For that reason a deacon is made by a bishop alone. Priests as well lay their hands on a priest, because of the like Spirit that the clergy share. But a priest is only able to receive it, he has no power to give it; therefore he does not ordain clergy: but at the ordination of a priest he indicates his agreement while the bishop ordains.

The prayer that follows, whose wording is poorly attested, emphasizes that the deacon is chosen to be a servant of the Church and to bring into the sanctuary that which the high-priest is to offer. This prayer can be interpreted as an encour-agement to the deacon—if he carries out his humble duties satisfactorily, he may be found worthy of a higher office.

The above diffuse and detailed passage gives the reader the impression that the ministry of deacons soon raised some difficult problems for the Church. The Eastern versions of the *Apostolic Tradition* all are expansive on this subject. On the one hand, following the line of the primitive document, they expound the limits of the deacon's functions and deny him every properly sacerdotal ministry; on the other, they encour-age him by recalling the great reward promised to those who serve the Lord in the persons of his brethren. The *Testamen-tum Domini* is particularly valuable in this respect. It dwells at length on the deacon's ministries; and it sees in him an expression, visible before the world of men, of a Church whose bishops and priests tend for their part to remain in the back-ground, devoting themselves to the contemplation of those divine mysteries which they have to preach by the word and show forth by the sacraments.

The various liturgies developed along similar lines. Begin-ning with the *Apostolic Constitutions*, they hold up Stephen, the First Martyr, as the example for all deacons to follow. The Syrian and Chaldean rites multiply prayers and hymns that set forth the graces of the diaconate. All rites pray with particular insistence that the Spirit may be poured out abundantly on those who are to receive this order, so that they may truly witness to Christ in all their varied duties and that through them every human adversity may be assuaged by those gifts of grace which are the sign of that messianic era which the prophets foretold.

The diaconal ministry still has considerable importance in the Eastern Churches. Especially in the Byzantine rite, deacons lead the people's prayer at public worship, and they are responsible for the good order of the church building and of the faithful. The priest is above all the pleader before God and the minister of his grace through the sacraments, and at the same time the spiritual father and counsellor of families and persons: deacons (particularly in non-Byzantine Churches) form an intermediate body between the laity, whose daily life they share and whose needs they know, and the priestly clergy with whom they are so closely associated at public worship.

LESSER MINISTERS

Deacons are helped in their duties by *subdeacons*, who in the East are numbered among the lesser ministers. However, the new code of Eastern canon law for Catholics has recently revived the legislation of the Emperor Justinian, whereby subdeacons are assimilated to deacons and priests in respect of inability to contract marriage after ordination.[4] In practice, the subdeacons of the Eastern Churches are more like the acolytes of the Roman tradition. All the Churches have an order of *readers*, whose office is to read the scriptural lessons at public worship, except the gospel and sometimes the Pauline epistle. The Syrian Church gives a special blessing to *singers* or psalmodists. The Armenians, both dissident and Catholic, have adopted all the lesser orders of the Western Church, that is, they have *doorkeepers*, *exorcists* and *acolytes* too.

---

[4] In all dissident and some Catholic Eastern Churches, a married man may be ordained deacon and priest.

Eastern rites provide more or less solemn services for the appointment to certain responsibilities between the priesthood and the episcopate. Some of these are simply administrative offices; but the Syrians, Maronites and Chaldeans have kept the institution of chorepiscopi, itinerant rural delegates of the bishop. However, like *archdeacon* or *archimandrite* without a monastic charge,[5] *chorepiscopus* is now little more than an honorary appellation. Rites for the election and enthroning of a *metropolitan* or a *patriarch* are of course on quite a different level. The forms for the consecration of a patriarch in the Syrian Pontificals, both Antiochene and Chaldean, are particularly well worth attention.

[5] In principle an archimandrite is the head of an important monastery; but first the Russians and then the Greeks adopted the practice of giving the name as a title of honour to unmarried priests; married Russian priests can be given the title of *archpriest* (cf. the extension of the title *abbé* in French-speaking countries since the eighteenth century).

CHAPTER IX

THE WEDDING LITURGY

The complexity and richness of wedding rites in Eastern Churches are in marked contrast with the businesslikeness—some would say the poverty—of the rite used today in the West. Such elaboration is no matter for surprise. Christian marriage is a sacrament: but it is nonetheless a social institution, deep-rooted in a society's tradition and culture. The Christian liturgy of marriage grew slowly, and to a considerable extent was made up of social customs of very long standing, purged, of course, of anything incompatible with Christian faith or morals. In the West, the ancient veiling of the bride was accompanied by a solemn blessing; later on, Germanic law gave first importance to the exchange of rings and the joining of hands. In the East, the last two became the rites characteristic of betrothal, while the crowning of bride and groom was regarded as the sacramental sign of their union. It is rather remarkable that, in spite of its late formation, the marriage ritual is in its essentials common to all the Churches of the East. We will, therefore, after glancing at its history, describe that of the Byzantine rite, noting any outstanding peculiarities in the other rites.

HISTORY AND DEVELOPMENT

Apart from a few rare injunctions, chiefly of Syrian origin, to Christians not to marry without referring the matter to their bishop, it is not till the end of the fourth century that the Church is found directly concerned in the marriages of the faithful: and even then it seems to have been only in an honorary sense. The contract of betrothal was simple and informal, and too easily broken, and it may be that the Church's influence contributed to the gradual substitution of a betrothal with earnest-money (Eastern in origin), ratified by the ring, the kiss and the hand-clasp of the couple. But these observances did not become part of the Church's liturgy before the eighth–ninth century, and probably were established first in Syria, where a special emphasis has been put on them down to our own day. The importance attached to matrimonial legislation by the Isaurian emperors (717–820) doubtless helped to spread the blessing of betrothals throughout the Byzantine empire, but it was only with the decrees of Leo VI the Wise at the end of the ninth century that this blessing entailed legal effects; and it was another two hundred years, under Alexis I Comnenus († 1118), before sanction was given to the already current practice of joining the betrothal contract with the liturgical blessing. This decision further increased the importance of the religious rite and strengthened its association with the office of crowning, in spite of Alexis's efforts to keep up a distinction between them, But there seemed no longer to be any reason for it now that the law recognized betrothal as a contract, though a purely civil one.

The solemn blessing of the bridal pair and the putting of a wedding crown on their heads by the priest were much earlier customs. In Egypt at the end of the fourth century it was the bishop or a priest who "gave away" the bride to the groom and joined their hands; and in other regions at about the same time it appears to have been the custom to invite the bishop to carry out this traditional duty of the father of a family. We learn from St Gregory Nazianzen and St John Chrysostom that in Cappadocia and at Antioch and Constantinople priests and bishops were often asked to impose the wedding-crown. The properly liturgical character of this observance is first attested in Armenia, when St Narses I the Great was catholicos (c. 364–c. 373).

This use of crowns, closely associated with heathen beliefs and practices, was rather repugnant to Christian sentiment, and it is understandable that bishops should have hesitated for some time before giving it their authority. The decisive turning-point came when St John Chrysostom gave it a high ascetical significance: "The crown that is put on the heads of bride and groom is a token of their victory: in that they have not succumbed to the lure of pleasure, they come undefeated to the haven of marriage. Why should one who, a slave to self-indulgence, has given himself up to harlots wear a crown? —for he has been defeated."[1] Chrysostom was familiar with the prayers that the priest used to say at the bride's home on the eve of a wedding; such was the custom in fervent families and he several times recommends it, but without, apparently, making it obligatory. In fact no council takes notice of the practice until the "Quinisextum" of 692, which confirmed the decrees of Timothy of Alexandria. Chrysostom's explanation of the crowning at a wedding was for a long time taken to imply forbiddance of second marriages.

So it was imperial authority and not the Church that took the initiative in considering as valid only those marriages which were concluded by a liturgical blessing. As a result of this decision, the blessing, and the crowning that went with it, came to be more and more widely regarded as constituting the sacrament; the more so because mutual consent seemed to be quite sufficiently expressed by the betrothal rites of exchanging rings and holding hands. Nevertheless it took another thousand years for this idea (alluded to by Pope St Nicholas I in his canonical letter to the Bulgars in 866) to be accepted as common theological teaching in the Byzantine Church. Down to the end of the nineteenth century there were many Eastern theologians who followed their Western brethren in seeing the essence of the marriage sacrament in the contractual act, but without bothering themselves with the question of "matter" and "form". But they were equally in agreement

[1] Homily ix, 2, *In epist. I ad Timotheum* (P.G. 62, col. 546).

that the liturgical rites are required for validity, and this requirement is expressly retained in the Catholic code of Eastern canon law.

THE BYZANTINE AND OTHER RITUALS

Except in the Chaldean rite where they are completely merged into one, all Eastern rites distinguish clearly between an office of betrothal, or "of the ring", and an office of marriage, or "of the crowning"; but to avoid the inconvenience arising from civil legislation which made betrothal an indissoluble contract, the two offices have for centuries normally been joined as a single rite. Some rites, including the Byzantine, have a special service, penitential in character, for the blessing of the rings at a second marriage, the crowning being in principle excluded.

The office of betrothal

This first part of the wedding rite is designed to take place after the eucharistic Liturgy, and it begins at the narthex or porch of the church, where the priest receives the bridal pair. After having asked them (in the Catholic ritual) if they are entering into their engagement freely, he blesses them, gives a lighted candle to each, and leads them through the nave to the sanctuary entrance. The office then begins with a litany which, after the usual petitions, asks that the couple may live in love, concord and faithfulness. Then come two prayers which are found in the most ancient existing manuscript and must be far older than that: "Everliving God, you who gather together what is scattered and have made the bond of love unbreakable, you who blessed Isaac and Rebecca and appointed them heirs of your promise, bless likewise these your servants and lead them in the way of holy living. For you are a merciful God and the lover of man. . . ." The second prayer is given additional solemnity by the invitation to "Bow your heads before the Lord": "Lord our God, you who have chosen that unstained virgin the Church to be your bride, bless this betrothal: join these your servants here in unity and keep them in peace and concord. . . ."

Since at least the tenth century, this prayer is followed by the exchange of rings between bride and groom: these rings, one of gold, the other of silver, have hitherto lain on the altar, to be hallowed by contact with it. Some rituals add other observances: the kissing of the bride's forehead by the groom, and especially the joining of their hands, which is found at Alexandria in the fourth century and became widely spread. This hand-clasp has particular importance among the Ruthenians (Ukrainians and others), who have given it the character of an oath on the gospels: the couple lay their joined hands on the gospel book, and the priest covers them with his stole, saying: "Let no man put apart those whom God has joined together. By the authority entrusted to me, I, God's unworthy servant, join you in holy marriage, and with Holy Church's authority I confirm and seal this union, in the name of the Father and of the Son and of the Holy Spirit. Amen." (This declaration was taken from the Polish ritual by the metropolitan Peter Mogila in the seventeenth century.) In current Byzantine practice the office is concluded by a long and diffuse prayer which rehearses various biblical allusions to rings. With some variations, this prayer figures in manuscripts from the end of the tenth century.

Even after these later elaborations the Byzantine ritual retains a comparative sobriety. It is not so in the Syrian, Coptic and Armenian Churches. In these, for instance, the bride's dowry of clothes, jewels, etc. is hallowed by a blessing. All Syrian Churches had the very ancient practice of ratifying the betrothal by the giving to the bride of a cross, to be worn round the neck. This is mentioned in a tenth-century Armenian Ritual as a characteristic betrothal observance and the Catholic Armenians still use the accompanying prayer, though the cross is no longer given. It has gone out of use among the Antiochene Syrians, but it was traditional in the thirteenth century, as the Nomocanon of Bar Hebraeus testifies; it can be traced at least to the same era among the Copts. On the other hand, there was originally in these rites only one ring, given to the bride by the groom or in his name. To the betrothal ring and cross the Chaldeans have added the shared loving-cup, which we shall find elsewhere at the end of the wedding proper.

The office of marriage

Since the time of Peter Mogila († 1646) the Ruthenians, under the influence of Western theology and liturgy, have emphasized the mutual consent of the parties to a marriage to a point where the rite of crowning is reduced to a mere appendage. But normally for all Easterners it is an essential element and the Catholic code of Eastern canon law expressly ratifies this tradition.

In the Byzantine rite, the office of crowning has immediately followed that of betrothal since the beginning of the eleventh century, if not longer. The bridal pair withdraw to the end of the church, and are conducted back processionally through the nave by the clergy; meanwhile Psalm 127 is sung, as was done at Christian weddings in the fourth century. Immediately after this procession the Russians have an explicit declaration of free consent from each party, and this is also found in some fifteenth-century Greek service-books; but the custom has never been adopted by the Orthodox as a whole.

As in all offices, the deacon sings the opening litany, whose special petitions are directed to the fertility of the home. The oldest documents follow it with a short prayer, which has since been overshadowed by two lengthy subsequent additions. The original prayer is:

Holy God, you made man out of the clay of the earth, and from his side you made woman and joined her with him as his helpmate, showing thereby that your lovingkindness would not have man to be alone in the world: from your holy dwellingplace, Master, stretch out now your hand and

join this man and this woman, your servants, for it is you
who unite man and woman. Give them agreement of minds,
crown them with love, make them one flesh, give fruitfulness
to their bodies, that they may find happiness in many children
and that their lives may be beyond reproach. For yours is the
power, the kingdom, the might and the glory, Father, Son and
Holy Spirit, now and always and for ever. Amen.

Then the priest put a crown on the bridegroom's head, one
also on the bride's, joined their hands, and blessed them with
this prayer:

Lord our God, in your work of salvation you were pleased
to show by your presence at Cana in Galilee that marriage
is to be held in honour: keep then, Master, in peace and concord these servants of yours whom you have joined one to
the other. May the dignity of their union be seen by all; watch
over their marriage-bed that it be not sullied and their whole
life that it be blameless, and make them worthy to reach a
prosperous old-age through keeping your commandments with
a pure heart. . . .

The service-book then refers to the blessing of the loving
cup, but without explicitly connecting it with the office of
crowning.

This first simplicity was rapidly lost: by the eleventh century it was overlaid by a whole service modelled on the
Liturgy of the Presanctified Gifts. It is still in use, but yet
more weighed down by two interminable prayers between the
litany and the old wedding prayer, "Holy God, you made
man . . .". These two prayers are patchworks of biblical
allusions, whose connecting thread it is difficult to trace: the
first refers to the weddings of the Hebrew patriarchs, making
use of scraps of information drawn from late Jewish sources,
and invokes for the bridal pair all the temporal blessings of
the Old Covenant; the second continues this theme, adding
those of divine protection and the crown of glory, with copious
examples. The crowning itself is accompanied by a rather
ambiguous formula, which could mean: "God's servant N.

receives as crown God's handmaid N., in the name of the
Father . . ."; or, more probably: "God's servant N. is crowned
for God's handmaid N . . .", and reciprocally. There follows
a liturgy of the word of the ordinary pattern: psalm verse
(20. 4–5), epistle (Ephesians 5. 20–33), gospel (John 2. 1–11);
short litany, ending with the old prayer of blessing, "Lord
our God, in your work . . ."; the litany before communion,
and the Lord's Prayer.

Nowadays, by a curious deviation, the ordinary custom is
not for the couple to receive holy communion but simply to
drink from a cup of wine, "the cup of fellowship", that the
priest blesses. Examination of old texts shows how this came
about. In accordance with an idea that has had a certain
popularity both in East and West, this wine was in the esti-
mation of some people "sanctified" by the mixing with it
of a fragment of the consecrated bread. Those who rejected
this theory had a celebration of the eucharistic Liturgy before
the wedding and kept the "presanctified" elements for the
communion of the bridal pair. Very occasionally mention
can be found of a real "wedding Mass", celebrated after the
crowning.

Nowadays, too, the drinking from the cup is followed by a
sort of wedding dance, in which the priest leads the couple
three times in a circle, the groom's man and bride's maid
holding the crowns above the heads of groom and bride respectively. The choir meanwhile sings two *troparia*: the first
is taken from the office of preparation for Christmas, apparently chosen because of its opening words that suggest a
joyful dance, rather than for its reference to the virgin birth;
the second is taken from the office of martyrs, because of
its allusion to a crown of glory. Finally, the crowns are
solemnly removed, and the priest says two prayers of blessing
over the newly-married couple.

In other Eastern Churches the office of crowning closely
resembles that of the Byzantine rite. The Armenians and
Ethiopians celebrate it during the eucharistic Liturgy. The

first-named have adapted from medieval Norman practice a threefold interrogatory concerning freedom of consent; this happens at the church door before the Liturgy begins, and the blessing and putting on of the crowns comes after the gospel. The Ethiopians also have an interrogatory that has perhaps been influenced by West-European usage (like the passages in the English wedding rite that derive from the Sarum use); this interrogatory is associated with the blessing and giving of the ring, while the blessing and putting on of the crowns comes at the communion.

It has been remarked that the Chaldeans have the loving-cup at that part of their service that corresponds to betrothal: the wine is blessed by dipping the cross in it and mixing in some *'henana* (cf. page 101), and the ring is blessed by dipping it into this mixture. With them the crowning seems originally to have taken place in the bride-chamber; it is lavishly accompanied by hymns and prayers. The Syrians give full importance to the procession after the crowning, and it makes its way to the room where the wedding-breakfast is to be eaten. The Copts have known several special customs from time to time. Till the middle of the nineteenth century bride and groom were anointed on forehead, breast and hands, and occasionally this is still done. In Egypt, and in Syria too, the family and domestic origins of the marriage ritual continue to be strongly marked, whereas in the Byzantine world the ceremonial influence of the imperial court has put the emphasis on the hierarchical side.

CHAPTER X

THE DIVINE OFFICE

The sanctifying by prayer of the principal times of day and night goes back to the beginning of Christianity and beyond them to Jewish tradition. However, it was some centuries before there was a fixed body of prayers adapted to the several hours, and in the definitive formation of the Divine Office the monks played a big part both in East and West. It was through them that the liturgies of all Churches acquired a night office, and others for the Third Hour (Terce; 9 a.m.), the Sixth Hour (Sext; midday) and the Ninth Hour (None; 3 p.m.). (These day-hours are wanting only in the archaic East Syrian rite; the Maronites did not have them till the eighteenth century.) Still, these offices were not a complete innovation. The *Apostolic Tradition* and Tertullian in the third century give plenty of information about the origin and significance of the prayer three times a day already prescribed in the *Didache*. Tertullian finds its origin in the apostolic age: the coming of the Holy Spirit at the third hour (Acts 2. 15); Peter's prayer and vision at the sixth hour (*ib*. 10. 9); Peter and John praying in the Temple at the ninth hour (*ib*. 3. 1.). The *Apostolic Tradition* associates these prayers with our Lord's passion: the crucifixion at the third hour, darkness over the earth at the sixth, Christ's death at the ninth; there are traces of this interpretation in several Eastern rites.

But the two most important times of prayer are dawn and twilight. These were the moments of solemn prayer in the synagogues, evocations of or substitutes for the sacrifices at morning and evening prescribed by the law of Moses. For Christians, praise at sunrise celebrates the glory of Christ's resurrection, while Vespers as the day dies recalls the taking down of his body from the cross and its burial for the Lord's Sabbath rest, with which death associates every Christian. That is why in the Chaldean rite long anthems in honour of the martyrs are sung at this moment every day.

As in the Roman rite, most Eastern rites have added special prayers for the beginning and end of the day—Prime and Complin; and the Armenians have an extra office, called the "Hour of Peace", between Vespers and Complin. At penitential seasons the Byzantine rite has "intermediate hours" between all the usual ones. But this rite has kept better than others the distinction between the Church's public Office and the Office of monks. The shortened vigil (*Pannukhis*) which is celebrated on Saturday evenings and the eves of feasts makes a close link between Vespers (*Hesperinos*) and the morning office (*Orthros*), which is at once followed by Prime. In parish churches the monastic psalmody is almost completely suppressed when it is of any length; so too are the long readings from the Fathers in the monastic *Pannukhis* which is celebrated dozens of times a year in big monasteries, such as those of Mount Athos—it lasts practically the whole night.[1]

STRUCTURE OF THE OFFICE

The Divine Office is everywhere made up of the same elements: psalms, hymns and anthems, litanies and prayers, and (generally in a secondary place) readings; but the arrangement of these elements varies greatly from rite to rite.

The Coptic Office and its close relative in Ethiopia have a place to themselves. Their structure, like that of the Roman Office, is fully monastic, that is to say, the essential element

---

[1] In the dissident Eastern Churches the clergy have no obligation to read the daily office privately. Local synods since 1736 have imposed this obligation on the Catholic clergy of some rites; in other rites the regulation is flexible or non-existent. [*Trans.*]

is the psalmody. Their peculiarity is that each hour involves
the recitation of twelve psalms, in accordance with the tradition that St Pachomius, the organizer of Egyptian monasticism, was so directed by an angel; whereas in general other
rites have the psalms in groups of three, at any rate in the
day-hours. The Coptic and Ethiopic rites also have a gospel
reading for each hour; but while the Copts make only a
limited use of hymns the Ethiopians have a superabundance
of them. One of their oddest forms is the "portrait" (*malke*),
a salutation (*salam*) addressed to each of the members of
Christ's body, or of our Lady's or other saint's. The "praises
of Mary" (*weddasie Maryam*) are specially abundant; they
originate in the Coptic *theotokia*, which in turn were doubtless
inspired by Syrian hymns. Among the Copts the *theotokion*
is sung between the *psali* (scriptural chant) and the anthem
of the day's saint. These local forms of hymnody are in
addition to the *troparia* taken from old Greek sources.

There is a large body of prayers and lyric stanzas (*troparia*)
to be found, more or less adapted, in the Syrian and Coptic
rites, as well as in the Byzantine and Armenian. The Copts
have sometimes even kept them partly in Greek. Whatever
their origin, these *troparia* are particularly important for the
Byzantine Office; indeed, they can be said to be its weft. They
occur between the final verses of the psalms of the principal
hours, and are then called *stikhera*; but they also occur in
isolation all over the Office, being named according to their
function and content. The concluding *troparion* of Vespers
and Lauds, called *apolytikion*, characterizes the feast and is
comparable to the antiphon at *Magnificat* and *Benedictus* in
the Roman Office; but it is given even more prominence, for
it is repeated in every hour, making a refrain for the whole
day.

The *troparia* sung between the verses of the eight or nine
biblical odes, which are the outstanding element of the Byzantine office of *Orthros*, are arranged so as to form a whole
harmonious poem, the *kanon*. Its history (which is referred

to on page 48 above) suggests that the Greek *kanon* is an adaptation of a Syrian form. Between the sixth and seventh odes of the *kanon* there are inserted a few strophes of the older *kontakia*, those great works of Christian poetry of which St Romanus the Singer was the master. Such exuberant developments of hymnody have lessened the place given to psalms and lessons. The continuous reading of the Psalter, divided into "sittings" (*kathismata*), is generally much shortened outside monasteries, where it originated; and the psalms and biblical canticles (odes) proper to each hour are themselves often abridged. They are cut down to the opening verses and those between which *stikhera* occur, and of the odes of the *kanon* only the *Magnificat* is still sung in its entirety. The biblical lessons are no longer read, except at Vespers on certain feasts and during Lent and Holy Week; at *Orthros* on Sundays one of eleven gospel passages referring to the Resurrection is read. In accordance with characteristic Byzantine usage, each office includes one or more diaconal litanies. During the opening psalmody at Vespers and *Orthros* the celebrant, wearing a stole (*epitrakhelion*) and standing before the middle doors of the screen, says a series of prayers of which some appear to be very ancient. After a litany, each office is ended by a prayer from the celebrant, during which all bow down, a dismissal formula and a blessing.

Hymnody has if anything an even greater part in the Syrian and Maronite Offices. The lyric and didactic pieces are of diverse origins and epochs, but from the earliest times it was characteristic of the Antiochene liturgy to give a big place to singing and processions, in order to satisfy a people whose religious devotion was very demonstrative. Short antiphons sung between the verses of psalms which soon grew into veritable poems (doubtless the origin of Byzantine *kanons*), and took the place of the psalms themselves; long and elaborate *troparia* which the patriarch Severus († 538) collected into the *Oktoekhos*, so called because the pieces were afterwards arranged according to the eight tones of Greek music: such was

the native Antiochene contribution, which later was enriched
by *kanons* translated from Greek into Syriac.

But the increasing use of Syriac for public worship in the
patriarchate of Antioch encouraged the adoption of hymns
from further east. These generally go under the name of the
Edessene deacon St Ephrem († *c.* 373), who gave rise to a
school of poet-theologians whose chief representatives were
Jacob of Sarug († 521) among the Jacobites and Narsai of
Nisibis († 507) among the Nestorians. Their compositions,
very varied in rhythmical pattern, spread far beyond the
Churches in which they originated; we have seen that, through
St Romanus the Singer and, less directly, the school of Mar
Saba, they had a strong influence on the development of
Byzantine hymn-writing.

Side by side with these hymns, whose arrangement is very
complex, the Syrian Office is characterized by a special form
of prayer, the *sedro*, which has already been mentioned when
discussing the eucharistic Liturgy. It is made up of a prologue
(*proemion*) of praise and a prayer of petition, which at Vespers (*Ramsho*) and morning prayer (*Sapro*) is followed by
a prayer with incense and a conclusion. Though its text is
sometimes found in the Byzantine Office, this *sedro* form is
peculiar to the Syrian Churches; it seems to derive from the
Jewish synagogues that were so numerous in eastern Syria.

Like the rest of the Armenian liturgy, its Divine Office
combines Syrian and Byzantine traditions; but the second
element has been more faithful to the early usages that at
Constantinople were supplanted by later ones; these were
due especially to the monks of Mar Saba and of the monastery of Studius, so that the rules of the Byzantine Office in
its existing form are in effect a set of monastic regulations.
So once again the Armenian rite is found to be a guide to
older practice; and this not only in the choice and arrangement of its parts, but in texts whose Greek original has been
lost or gone out of use. The Armenian Office has a large
number of hymns of its own, notable for the quality of their

poetic and musical expression as well as for teaching value. The great Armenian hymn-writer was the catholicos St Narses IV the Gracious († 1172), who reorganized both his Church and its liturgy. No doubt he made use of many earlier compositions, in the same way that succeeding ages made use of his.

The Chaldean Office is marked by antiquity and sobriety. It has never included the hours of Terce, Sext and None, and the Catholic monks have had to borrow them from the Maronites. It gives first place to psalmody more than does any other Eastern Office, not excluding the Coptic; and it has the common arrangement of dividing the Psalter into twenty sections (*hullale*), each subdivided into two or three "sittings" (*marmitha*). But whereas elsewhere this monastic type of psalmody has been more or less smothered by hymn-singing, it has kept its primary importance among the East Syrians. It is accompanied by characteristic antiphons (*onitha*) between the psalm verses, the finest and most important being those of the martyrs at *Ramsha* and *Sapra*; these are a daily reminder of the great persecution by the Persian Shapur II during the fourth century. We shall see later how restricted the Chaldean "sanctoral" is, but in fact the memory of these great witnesses to Christ is at the very heart of East Syrian daily prayer.

Other characteristic features of this rite are the outstanding place of the Lord's Prayer, which begins each hour and every other liturgical office; the "collects", often full of doctrine, which go with each division of the Psalter; and the short phrases inserted between the first and last verses of psalms to indicate their Christian application. At *Ramsha* and *Sapra*, as at the beginning of the eucharistic Liturgy, there is sung during the censing a hymn peculiar to this rite called *Lakhu Mara*: "Lord of all, we confess you. Jesus Christ, we glorify you. For you give life to our bodies, you are the Saviour of our souls." In spite of its length, the night-office in this Church is observed not only by monks but also by some laymen; for this purpose they are sometimes grouped into confraternities, whose members are given the title of deacon (*shammas*). Here we see the continuance of an organ of the Christian community that goes back to the earliest ages, before monks had come into existence.

THE HALLOWING OF TIME

The day

The first aim of the arrangement of the Divine Office is to provide for the sanctification of the principal times of day and night. We have seen that at an early date each of these was associated with the memory of a moment in our Redeemer's passion; and in some Churches the chief stages of man's creation and fall were added as a sort of background. The evening and morning offices, in direct continuity with those of the Jewish synagogue, were specially devoted to this celebration of the creation, and it was the synagogue that determined the choice of psalms, some of which are the same in nearly all liturgies and represent usage that is extremely ancient, perhaps prechristian: Psalms 140–141 at Vespers; Psalms 50 (penitential), 62 (early morning), 148–150 (Lauds), as well as the first canticle of Moses (Exod. 15. 1–19, a paschal theme) and the canticle of the young men in the furnace (Dan. 3. 57–88, a praise of God as creator and deliverer) at the morning office. This continuity with the synagogue is still more striking if the last part of the office, with its saying of the *Trisagion* and the Lord's Prayer, may be considered a Christian transposition of the *Tefilla* (solemn prayer of blessing) and the *Kedusha* (the Trisagion of Isaias, 6. 3), the oldest attested nucleus of the synagogue prayers. Prayers proper to each rite amplify the same theme.

In the Byzantine and Coptic rites this daily structure of the Office is of the first importance, and the essential book for its celebration is the *Horologion*; the collections of hymns proper to each day of the week, to Lent and Eastertime and to feasts on fixed dates are only a supplement—though a considerable one—to be inserted in an unchanging framework. But in the Armenian and all the Syrian rites there is a proper Office for every day of the week.

The week

The second element in the sanctification of time is the week. In the Old Testament the passing of a week marks the rhythm of the Creation; for Christians it is the period of the recurring celebration of the Lord's Passover, of the triumph of the risen Christ over sin and death. Sunday as a feast of the resurrection is very marked in Eastern liturgies. In every rite the various texts proper to Sunday play on this theme and draw out its cosmic significance, an aspect rather forgotten in the West where Sunday, the day of Christian assembly, has become the occasion for a liturgical catechesis extending over the whole year. The Byzantine rite above all recognizes the paschal aspect of every Sunday in very striking fashion. At the morning office it retains the practice, recorded at Jerusalem in the fourth century, of reading a Resurrection gospel, for which in the tenth century the emperor Leo VI composed eleven *troparia* relevant to the passages read and now sung after them. As well as the odes of the *kanon*, the *stikhera* and the other *troparia*, several other texts proper to Sunday acclaim the Anointed One who "overcame death by death and gave life to those who were in the grave." There are similar expressions in other rites, particularly the Armenian, though in none of them is the Easter theme so exclusive as among the Byzantines. The Syrian and Armenian rites, for instance, also emphasize the Church, always a preoccupation of the Syrian tradition.

Friday and, to a lesser degree, Wednesday are generally sacred to the memory of the Cross. Among the Armenians this commemoration overrides any other feast, and they dedicate Wednesday to the Annunciation, when the work of our redemption was begun. Among the East Syrians, on the other hand, Friday is the day reserved for the rare feasts of

saints which they observe. This apparent exception is explained by the fact that the *cultus* of saints was at first
exclusively a *cultus* of martyrs, and it seemed appropriate
to join the commemoration of their witness by violent death
to the commemoration of the saving Cross that they showed
forth in their own bodies.

The significance of the other days of the week is less clearly
marked. But it gradually became customary, especially in the
Byzantine rite, to dedicate each to the memory of a group of
holy ones: Monday to the angels, Tuesday to St John the
Forerunner, who summed up in himself all the holy men,
patriarchs and prophets, of the Old Covenant, Thursday to
the Apostles, Saturday, in a predominantly mourning office,
to all the other saints, especially the martyrs. The *troparia*
proper to each of these groups have their equivalents in the
East Syrian rite and in the Armenian night office. It is, however, not easy to find any special attribution in the *psali* proper
to each day of the week in the Coptic morning office, to which
the Ethiopians add a hymn to our Lady, also proper to each
day.

The year

The organization of the cycle of the liturgical year seems
to have begun in Jerusalem in the time of St Cyril († 386),
but it developed differently in different Churches, nowhere
more rigidly than among the East Syrians. It is their catholicos
Ishu'yab III who is supposed to have divided the year into
periods, on a basis of seven weeks each, one or other of which
is omitted according to the year: namely, Dedication of the
church and the Annunciation, Epiphany, Lent, Easter, the
Apostles, Summer, Elias and the Cross, Moses. Some of these
appellations are taken from feasts falling within the relevant
period. Other Churches were not so rigid. The West Syrians
divide the year into seven periods: Dedication and Annunciation, Christmas, Epiphany, Lent and the Passion, Easter, Pentecost, the Cross (after September 14). But whereas the East

Syrians begin the ecclesiastical year on December 1, that is, between the four Sundays of the Dedication and the four Sundays of the Annunciation, the West Syrians make it correspond with the normal beginning of the liturgical year, that is, with November 1, near the first of the two Dedication Sundays observed in their rite.

The importance given to the very ancient feast of the Dedication[2] emphasizes from the very beginning of the liturgical year that mystery of the Church which continually recurs in Syrian piety and theology. It will be noticed, too, that their tradition soon developed (between 350 and 600) a period of preparation for Christmas, called "of the Annunciation". It covers four Sundays among the East and six among the West Syrians, and is marked by the reading of "annunciation" gospels: to Zachary and to Mary before the birth of John the Baptist and (among the West Syrians) to Elizabeth when Mary visited her, and to Joseph. It is an almost universal custom to read the genealogy of Jesus according to St Matthew on the last Sunday before Christmas.

The Armenians have a very special liturgical cycle, which is twofold. One, whose dates are very variable, is governed by the feast of Easter, with ten weeks of preparation and fourteen after it, the latter divided into seven before Whit Sunday and the seven after. The other cycle begins on the feast of the Falling Asleep of Mary on the Sunday nearest August 15, and its centre is the feast of the Cross on the Sunday nearest September 14; it lasts twenty-two weeks, of which the last six or seven are a preparation for the Theophany (Epiphany: January 6), which was primitively the only

[2] No doubt the Palestinian feast of the "dedication of all the altars in the world", substituted with polemic intent for the Jewish feast of the *Encaenia*, the anniversary of the dedication of the Temple at Jerusalem, which was celebrated in December. Later on this feast would be anticipated by a month because of the development of the time of preparation for Christmas. Cf. B. Botte in *L'Orient Syrien* II, pp. 65–70 (Paris 1957).

feast on a fixed date in the Armenian calendar. The Armenian Church is the only one that has never adopted the separate feast of Christmas on December 25.[3]

The weeks between the octave of the Theophany and the beginning of the paschal cycle and those between the end of the latter and the Sunday nearest August 15 are called the Time of the Theophany and the Time of the Transfiguration respectively, from the feast kept on the first Sunday of the period; they are devoted especially to the commemorations of saints, which are very rare at other times.

The Byzantine and Coptic temporal cycles are far less elaborate for they take no account of fixed feasts. The Copts have a period of preparation for Christmas, with special offices in honour of our Lady (*Theotokia* for the month of Kihak), but the Byzantines have a special cycle only in preparation for Easter and at paschaltime. The important body of relevant hymns fills two books: the *Triodion*, whose definitive arrangement is credited to the Studite monks in the ninth century, for the first period, and the *Pentekostarion*, originating at Mar Saba in Palestine, for the second.

The *Triodion* in particular repays careful study. The Sunday offices in preparation for Easter elaborate a fundamental Christian view of man and the world, and parts of them are reproduced in the Armenian rite. The Sundays before Lent call to mind the Pharisee and the Publican and the Prodigal Son, types of what should be the state of mind of man the sinner; then the Last Judgement is recalled, and the first sin that banished mankind from the garden of happiness. Twice during Lent itself the penitential Great *Kanon* of St Andrew of Crete is sung, setting out with much biblical imagery man's state of sin and penitence. As in all liturgies, the unfolding of the various aspects of the process of salvation culminates during the great week, called Passion Week in the East, before Easter Sunday; the biblical readings, rather

[3] The small minority of Catholic Armenians has adopted this feast. [*Trans.*]

infrequent during the year, commoner in Lent, are now un-broken. The Coptic rite has many evidences of a "continuous reading", beginning with Genesis after the eucharistic Liturgy on Palm Sunday and finishing with the Apocalypse on Holy Saturday. With the Byzantines, the continuous reading of the four gospels is provided for during the earlier days of the week; and at the night-office between Maundy Thursday and Good Friday the narrative of the Passion is read in twelve sections, with *troparia* between them. There are similar observances in the other rites, wherein the night of Easter also has long readings; but the Byzantines now anticipate this ancient vigil on Saturday morning, and at midnight have a short morning office, preceded by a procession and followed by the eucharistic Liturgy. During this office the Paschal *Kanon* attributed to St John Damascene is sung: it seems to be a development of very ancient *troparia* sung during a procession at the holy places in Jerusalem. One other rite common to all Eastern Churches deserves mention: the "kneeling office" at Vespers of Pentecost. In virtue of a decree of the Council of Nicaea, kneeling is forbidden throughout paschal-time. On the evening of Whit Sunday, the coming of the Holy Spirit is solemnly besought in three prayers which are said by celebrant and people on their knees.

THE CULTUS OF THE SAINTS

The cycle of time, daily, weekly and yearly, shows and ensures that natural time belongs to the order of salvation. Through a number of outstanding figures, the commemora-tion of saints brings before us the process of salvation work-ing itself out in human history. In this matter, as in so many others, the Eastern Churches are conservative and traditionalist, and their calendars of saints became fixed very early: those of the non-Byzantine Churches show hardly a name later than the sixth century. In the Orthodox churches, the common calendar was stabilized at the commemoration of the great heroes of the struggle against Iconoclasm in the eighth–ninth century. Since then the theologian Gregory Palamas († 1359) has been given a place of honour in the liturgical year; he is looked on as a new and final witness to the Orthodox belief in man's deification by grace as a consequence of God's incarnation. He is honoured on the second Sunday in Lent, the first Sunday having since 843 been observed as a commemoration of the victory of orthodoxy by the vindication of the veneration of holy images. But the Russians have cast their net wider and, following Rome's example, have adopted a procedure of canonization, while maintaining the legitimacy of a *cultus* grounded on general custom, for they consider the consensus of Christian people to be an expression of the Church's faith. The Catholic Churches have in varying degrees enriched their calendars with feasts adopted from the West, at the same time suppressing those of people who are accounted heterodox, and sometimes, more arbitrarily, of those who lived since the presumed time of separation from Catholic unity.

The various Eastern Churches give a more or less large place to the *cultus* of "Old Testament saints". This seems to have originated in the yearly commemoration of the dedication of churches built in honour of such persons in places connected with them, such as Mount Nebo for Moses, Hebron for the Patriarchs and David, or some mountain or other for Elias.[4] The influence of Palestinian monks at Constantinople and the desire to make the imperial city a sort of Holy Land also led to the building of such churches and the spread of the *cultus* of holy men of the Old Covenant.

But in every Church the foundation of its calendar of saints is the martyrs whom it particularly venerates either because

[4] Through a play on his name (*helios* in Greek means "sun") and because of his taking-up in a fiery chariot, Elias, as also our Lady and John the Baptist, was chosen as the Christians' patron of temples and high places formerly considered sacred to the sun. These sanctuaries were specially numerous in the highlands of Greece, Crete and Lebanon.

they lived or were martyred within its borders or because their
fame was carried far and wide by pilgrims or others. To these
were added in time great doctors and bishops, the guardians
and teachers of the faith, and outstanding monks and nuns,
whose life of prayer and penance was everywhere looked on
as a kind of martyrdom.

Especially from the tenth century, the Byzantine calendar
of saints became more and more ecumenical,[5] taking in the
more famous saints of all parts of the empire, including re-
covered Syria and Armenia, but in the other Churches it is
much more strictly localized. This is pushed to an extreme in
the Coptic Church, which honours Egyptian saints to the
exclusion of almost all others, and the East Syrian Church,
whose calendar contains less than fifty saints' names—with a
few exceptions, the particular feast of a saint or group of
saints occurs only on a Friday. The Armenian Church, which
has saints' feasts on Mondays, Tuesdays, Thursdays and
Saturdays, observes those of certain Syrians and Cappa-
docians, as well as its own Armenians. The West Syrian
sanctoral is more extensive, but there are very few proper
offices; the commemoration generally consists simply of the
reading of the pertinent entry in the *Synaxarion*, a sort of
expanded martyrology that is found in all Eastern Churches.
Most of these Churches also observe feasts of the fathers
assembled at certain great councils of the Church.

The cycle of feasts of the Blessed Virgin Mary varies from
Church to Church. The oldest, observed by them all, is that
of August 15th; it is attested at Jerusalem soon after the
Council of Ephesus in 431, but only later became the feast of
her Falling Asleep (*koimesis*); the feast of her Birthday on
September 8th is also very widely observed. On the other
hand, her Conception (December 8th or 9th) and her Presen-

---

[5] This concept of ecumenicity, in the strict sense of the word which
restricts it to the world in relation with the Roman empire, was
strengthened and given depth by the patriarch Photius († 895) in his
Epanogogue on the fellowship of different peoples in their confession
of the lordship of Christ.

tation in the Temple (November 21st) were at first proper to
the Byzantine rite, and were introduced elsewhere through
Western influence. The Annunciation (March 25th) and the
Presentation of Jesus in the Temple (February 2nd) are everywhere treated as feasts of our Lord, like Christmas or the
Epiphany. Every rite has certain proper feasts of Mary: the
Syrian tradition celebrates her at seed-time, harvest and
vintage, and such special feasts are notably numerous among
the Copts and Byzantines, especially the Russians. Some of
these feasts are associated with a shrine or an icon.

The collections of hymns and other elements proper to the
offices of fixed date are sometimes voluminous: the Byzantine
Menaia run to a volume for each month, the printed Syrian
Fanqit is in seven volumes, and no doubt a complete edition
of the Chaldean *Gazza* would be little less. The Coptic *Difnar*
and Armenian *Sharakan* are not so expansive.

THE CHURCH AND ITS DEDICATION

The *cultus* of saints, of the martyrs above all, leads us to
say a few words in conclusion about the dedication of
churches, and particularly of altars, which was often the
starting-point of this observance.

Not that, in the Eastern Churches, the presence of relics of
saints is a constitutive element in the dedication of a church
building, as it has been for so long in the Roman tradition.
The Byzantine ritual for consecrating an altar includes, at the
end, the placing at its base of a small casket containing relics;
and in the same liturgy the Eucharist is normally celebrated
on an *antimension*, an altar-cloth into which a few tiny saints'
relics are sewn and on which an image of Christ's burial is
depicted. The Syrian ritual for consecrating churches also provides for the depositing of relics in some suitable spot, but
this is not essential to the consecration.[6] But the rite that is

[6] The Syrian and Coptic rites use as portable altars wooden boards
that have been consecrated by anointing with *myron*.

universal in the East, and the only one used by Chaldeans and
Copts, for the dedication of a church is the anointing of the
newly-built altar with *myron* or with an oil consecrated for
this purpose. In the Byzantine rite this setting-up of the altar,
reserved to the bishop, is regarded as one of the most important parts of the ceremony. It is clear that the anointing of
the church walls is only an extension of that of the altar.

But the dedication formularies used in the various rites and
the commentaries written on them, especially in Syria and at
Constantinople—commentaries which in their turn have
strongly influenced church construction and decoration—are
in unanimous agreement that the church building is a visible
expression of the community that meets in it, and that this
community is built on the foundation of the Apostles and the
bishops who succeed them, and of those great witnesses the
martyrs, and the monks who are heirs to their prophetical
mission. The Syrian and Armenian Churches have introduced
at the beginning of the eucharistic Liturgy hymns which evoke
this mystery of the Church very finely; and the Dedication
Sundays which begin the Syrian liturgical year provide the
opportunity further to develop its aspects, above all to acclaim
the Church as bride and mother, whose jewels are the martyrs
and saints.

In Byzantine tradition the mystery of the Church is expressed chiefly by the icons. The canonical decoration of
church buildings, as fixed since the defeat of Iconoclasm,
expresses it most fully, whether on the iconostasis or on the
walls of narthex and nave; the upper part is normally given
over to icons of saints. On the iconostasis they are in the
attitude of supplication, turned towards Christ to whom his
Mother and John the Forerunner are appealing (*deesis*). The
procession on the nave walls is directed towards the apse of
the sanctuary, which since the eighth century often bears an
image of our Lady, her hands raised in prayer, bearing a
medallion of Christ whom she offers for the worship of the
angels, the saints and the faithful: this icon of the Mother of

God (*Theotokos*) is a figure of the Church. Below the *deesis* our Lord is often represented giving communion to the Apostles and being served by angels as deacons: this Heavenly Liturgy completes the symbolical expression of the mystery of the Church. These icons are part and parcel of the celebration, and exceedingly important for the understanding of the Orthodox faith. For, even more in the East than in the West, this faith is most fully lived and experienced in this world in the act of the liturgical celebration; this, under the veil of sacramental signs, anticipates the divine realities which, having now an earnest of them, we look forward with sure hope to knowing in their fullness in time to come. As Father Sergius Bulgakov says, "The Liturgy is Heaven on earth".

SELECT BIBLIOGRAPY

Srawley, J. H.: *The Early History of the Liturgy*, Cambridge University Press, and New York, Macmillan, 1947.

Brightman, F. E.: *Liturgies Eastern and Western*. Vol. 1, Eastern, Oxford University Press, 1896.

Attwater, D. *The Christian Churches of the East,* 2 vols., London, Duckett, and Milwaukee, Bruce, 1948.
Eastern Catholic Worship, London, Duckett, and New York, Devin-Adair, 1945. English versions of the main parts of the eucharistic Liturgies.

King, A. A.: *The Rites of Eastern Christendom*, 2 vols, London, Burns & Oates, 1950.

Salaville, S.: *An Introduction to the Study of Eastern Liturgies* (translated from the French by Mgr J. M. T. Barton), London, Sands, 1938.

The Divine Liturgy of . . . John Chrysostom, London, Burns & Oates, 1926. The most usual Byzantine eucharistic Liturgy, text in Greek and English, with notes by Dom P. de Meester (translated by the Benedictines of Stanbrook).

The Byzantine Liturgy, London, Duckett, and New York, Fordham Russian Center, 1956. The Chrysostom and Basil Liturgies, translated by Fr C. C. Englert, Russian usage.

Nassar, S.: *Book of Divine Prayers and Services*, New York, Blackshaw Press, 1938. The Liturgy and offices for all Sundays and many other days, translated from the Orthodox books.

Raya, J. and de Vinck, J.: *Byzantine Missal*, Birmingham, Ala., St George's Church. The Chrysostom and Basil Liturgies in English, with the Sunday "propers" and some sacramental and other offices. Catholic Melkite usage.

The Byzantine services for Epiphany, Holy Week and Pentecost and the rites of baptism, marriage and anointing have been published separately, in Greek and English, by Williams & Norgate (Ernest Benn Ltd), London.

A Manual of Eastern Orthodox Prayers, London, S.P.C.K., and New York, Macmillan, 1945. Taken from Byzantine liturgical sources.

The Akathistos Hymn (translated by Vincent McNabb), Oxford, Blackfriars Publications, 1947. A Byzantine office in honour of our Lady.

NEALE, J. M.: *Hymns of the Eastern Church*, London, J. T. Hayes, 1882.

ZVEGINTZOV, C.: *Our Mother Church: Her Worship and Offices*, London, S.P.C.K., 1948. A simple practical explanation of the Byzantine liturgy, written for Russian Orthodox.

WOOLLEY, R. M.: *Coptic Offices*, London, S.P.C.K., and New York, Macmillan, 1930. Translation of the rites of baptism and confirmation, marriage, anointing the sick and burial.

CODRINGTON, H. W.: *Studies of the Syrian Liturgies*, Oxford, Newman Bookshop, and New York, C.N.E.W.A., 480 Lexington Avenue, 1952.

KOROLEVSKY, C.: *Living Languages in Catholic Worship* (translated by D. Attwater), London and New York, Longmans, 1957.

RICE, D. TALBOT: *Byzantine Art*, London and Baltimore, Penguin, 1954.

HAMILTON, J. A.: *Byzantine Architecture and Decoration*, London, Batsford, 1956.

The Music for the Liturgy of St John Chrysostom (according to Russian usage), Tournai, Desclée, n.d.

Eastern Churches Quarterly, Oxford, Newman Bookshop, and New York, C.N.E.W.A., 480 Lexington Avenue. This Catholic periodical was founded by Dom Bede Winslow, monk of Ramsgate, in 1936; it is now edited by Dom Edmund Jones.